THE SEE SERIES

ROMANS

A DEVOTIONAL COMMENTARY

CHRIS TIEGREEN

See God's purposes with new eyes

Visit Tyndale online at tyndale.com.

Visit Tyndale Momentum online at tyndalemomentum.com.

Tyndale, Tyndale's quill logo, *Tyndale Momentum*, and the Tyndale Momentum logo are registered trademarks of Tyndale House Ministries. Tyndale Momentum is a nonfiction imprint of Tyndale House Publishers, Carol Stream, Illinois.

Romans: A Devotional Commentary: See God's Purposes with New Eyes

Designed by Dean H. Renninger

Published in association with the literary agency of Mark Sweeney and Associates, Carol Stream, Illinois.

For information about special discounts for bulk purchases, please contact Tyndale House Publishers at csresponse@tyndale.com, or call 1-855-277-9400.

ISBN 978-1-4964-8545-8

Printed in India

31 30 29 28 27 26 25
7 6 5 4 3 2 1

For Christopher

Contents

The See Series

Human beings live by vision. We're directed by the images in our minds. We pursue goals when we can *see* them; we grow according to examples we've observed more than the knowledge we've learned; and we embrace hope, despair, and numerous other perspectives based on what we see happening around us. Even people who don't think of themselves as visionary tend to have some mental picture of where they are headed and why. It's the way we're wired.

Most of us have a big vision—a sense of ultimate meaning and destiny, or even just a dream or a goal for our lives. We want to live with purpose. We orient our lives by what we can picture.

We also have smaller visions—what's on the agenda for today, this week, this year, or even the next couple of decades—that shape our short-term decisions.

If our little visions and big vision don't align with each other, we feel frustrated and compromised, as if our lives are going nowhere and our desires may never be fulfilled. But if we can align these visions and see clearly, we grow steadily, even dramatically, into our purpose and calling.

SEE, BE, LIVE

Christian teaching hasn't always recognized our visionary nature. Much instruction over the years has been based on a know-it-then-do-it approach to Scripture—as if life change were simply a matter of learning the truth and applying it. But such an approach bypasses heart transformation and can easily become legalistic and frustrating.

Though knowing and doing are both very important, following Jesus is more than a matter of knowledge and willpower. We can never *will* ourselves to be who we need to be. We are not called simply to *do*; we are called to *be*. When we put knowing and doing before being, we end up in the same condition that many of the scribes and Pharisees of Jesus' time found themselves in—as pious people aiming to live godly lives without the necessary inner transformation.

Let me explain what I mean by *knowing*—an unfortunately imprecise word in English. We might read the Bible and *know* the commandments, instructions, encouragement, and truth it conveys. We receive that information and even agree with it. And if we want to be obedient, we will act on what we know. In that sense, our approach is both cognitive and behavioral—our thoughts affect our actions. But knowledge alone won't change our hearts, motives, desires, impulses, and everything else in us that needs to be transformed.

We see this phenomenon in the multitudes of people who memorize Jesus' words about faith but still lie awake all night with worry; who love Psalm 23 but still believe they are pursued by misfortune, not goodness and mercy; who agree that Jesus is Lord but don't live as though he is. Knowledge and action alone aren't comprehensive and compelling enough to reshape us.

In addition to our intellectual or informational knowledge, we also live from a particular worldview that shapes everything about us. This, too, is *knowing*, but it's a radically different kind of knowledge, isn't it? It's how we see the world, which is why I prefer words such as *seeing* and *vision* to capture it. This kind of knowledge goes well beyond information and instructions. It reflects not only *what* we know but also *how* we know and how we *respond* (perhaps even unconsciously) to what we know. It forms our sense of identity and becomes the filter for every piece of information we receive. Whereas the first kind of knowing may shape our *thoughts* to a degree, this kind shapes our *thought processes* (and therefore our thoughts) to a greater degree.

For example, if I dive into a lake or ocean and swim around for an hour or two, I experience something of marine life. I can practice different strokes, get used to holding my breath for longer periods, and work on distances and techniques. I *know* swimming. I might even start to think I swim like a fish. But if I'm a fish, moving around in the water is my nature. I don't even have to think about strokes or breath or what it takes to live in the water. I just do it. I know swimming without even knowing that I know it. It's part of who I am.

God has given us a new nature and called us to live from it. It's a radical transformation—so radical that we aren't quite sure how to do it. Many of us turn back to old paradigms, trying to live out our new life by reforming our old nature. We try to make the new ways "natural," often by disciplining ourselves to conform to what we believe is true. In other words, we *know* and *do* by receiving information and acting on it.

But what if we really saw ourselves as new creations and gave no thought to any other possibility? What if it never even occurred to us that God might not be working in all the circumstances of our lives? What if love and worship were the default settings of our lives and we were shocked by anything else that came out of our hearts? What if our new nature was . . . well, natural?

There is no flip of a switch that gets us there, but some ways are better than others. I've experienced the futility of self-discipline born of knowing and doing (which, again, though insufficient, are still important). But I've also experienced the transformation that comes from that second kind of knowing—the radical reorientation of a worldview that shapes everything about us.

I call this radical reorientation *seeing* because we often express this deeper, more comprehensive knowledge in visual terms.

"I know you told me this would work, but I didn't *see* how."

"I knew she cared, but now I *see* how much."

"You can argue with me all you want, but the way I *see* it . . ."

We instinctively know there's a seeing that goes deeper than informational knowledge, and this seeing transforms vital elements of our personality—our hopes and dreams; our gut feelings; our deeply rooted attitudes, instincts, and motives. Knowing information and responding to it may or may not change our heart. A radically new perspective does.

Embracing a new worldview may be catapulted forward by visual or sensory knowledge, or by seeing in a new way. They say a picture is worth a thousand words—a *million* seems closer to the mark—and is far more memorable. That's why the Bible is full of stories, parables, and experiences; why God inspired prophets to see visions and illustrate truth in tangible ways; and why he eventually clothed himself in human flesh to live among us. From beginning to end, God gives us images—highly visual and symbolic representations of who he is and what he does. We don't just read his instructions; we see what living out the truth looks like. We don't just read that he is a deliverer; we see numerous examples of dramatic deliverance. He doesn't just tell us he cares for us; he inspires a king to portray him as a shepherd and his Son to dramatize sacrificial, unconditional love in eternally indelible ways. Those pictures and portrayals are life changing.

If how we live flows out of who we are, being must come before doing. And if *seeing* so profoundly shapes *being*, then having this life-changing vision is vital. It is the key to the transformation we long for—that is, we become what we behold. The Holy Spirit works powerfully on the screens of our minds. We are drawn to whatever we focus on and emulate what we admire. Discipleship that begins with vision flows much more naturally into being and doing. Vision stirs us to be who we're called to be and to live as we're called to live.

The significance of our vision is the premise behind this devotional commentary series. The goal is to embrace a holistic, visual mode of learning. This series assumes that because we, as human beings, live from our identity and follow whatever vision we have, transformation happens by seeing in new ways. Instead of encouraging us simply to *know* and then *do*, the aim of these commentaries is to cast a vision for us to *see*, then *be*, then *live*. Like Jesus, who incorporated visual language into all his teaching, this series aims to refocus our inner eye. If we can see what the biblical writers saw and live according to that vision, we can be transformed.

THE ART OF ENVISIONING

We must train our brains to see and think in new ways. It doesn't just happen. The biblical mandate to renew our minds implies a conscious reorientation of our thought life. Old thought patterns are stubborn; those established neural pathways actively resist new pathways as intruders (which is why New Year's resolutions, exercise and diet plans, and quitting a bad habit can be so difficult). In most areas of life, this neurological dynamic—tapping into our established neural pathways—is helpful; we don't have to relearn everything each day. But when we've been called to reorient the way we think, we have to be relentless about it.

At a practical level, we can greatly amplify this process by (1) recognizing the vision behind biblical texts; (2) immersing ourselves in that vision (declaring the truths of Scripture out loud can help with this, as our brain is very responsive to the sound of our own voice, even if, at first, we don't think we sound convincing); and (3) practicing the art of envisioning.

This latter practice has been somewhat disparaged over the past couple of centuries because we've associated it with "imagination"—as in, "that's *only* your imagination," or "that's just a figment of your imagination," as if our internal vision is no reflection of reality. This would be news to biblical prophets, psalmists, storytellers, and teachers of parables, who all used highly visual language to express truth. Our imagination *can* be used to disengage us from reality—in fact, that's what many people do with it—but it is also our primary means of envisioning truth, which is exactly why God gave us so many stories and images and illustrations. He *wants* us to see his Kingdom—to picture his nature, his purposes, and his work in our lives. It's impossible to read Jesus' parables, study the stories in Acts or in the Old Testament historical books, or read the Psalms and Prophets without developing certain images in our minds. Our lives change when we immerse ourselves in those images.

In envisioning the Kingdom of God and all God's ways, we aren't trying to convince ourselves of something that *isn't* true—simply a figment of our imagination. We're training ourselves in what *is*. Sanctified imagination is not a flight from reality; it's a flight directly into it. We insist that our natural minds, long steeped in limited vision and distorted ways of thinking, must now conform to reality as God defines it.

That's when transformation occurs. When we see God, ourselves, our world, and his Kingdom as he does, we rarely have to discipline ourselves to live differently. We just do it.

IN THIS COMMENTARY

Because this is a *devotional commentary*, you will find material here that fits both descriptors: commentary on the text, and devotional or inspirational thoughts that apply the text to your life, specifically in the ways you see, become transformed, and live out that transformation. In this commentary, you will find

- an introduction to the biblical book
- an introduction for each subsection of the book, explaining its place and purpose in the text, the context or background of that section, and how it fits into the big-picture vision of biblical truth
- a series of devotionals on the text that
    - further explain context, background, meaning, and purpose
    - offer suggestions for practical application
    - inspire and challenge you to *re-envision*—to learn to see in new ways
- a discussion guide in the back to help you further reflect on the Scripture passages and talk about them with others to expand your spiritual vision even more

As you read, practice the art of envisioning. Pray for Holy Spirit–inspired perspectives. Notice what and how the biblical writers see, and immerse your heart and mind in those visions. Adopt them as your own. More and more, you will enter into the heights and depths of God's Kingdom and live in his ways.

INTRODUCTION TO ROMANS

Paul had spent years evangelizing the eastern Mediterranean—Asia Minor and the Aegean rim—and now he turned his eyes further west. Fully embracing his identity as "apostle to the Gentiles" (11:13), he wanted to go to Rome and then on to Spain (15:24). Generally he wrote letters to churches he had founded and nurtured, but the church at Rome was different. It was at the hub of the empire, the seat of influence, an irresistible pull for someone like Paul. Though he hadn't yet been to Rome, he knew people there, and those connections were the only open door he needed.

The timing and occasion of many of Paul's letters make for interesting debate among New Testament scholars, but this one seems pretty straightforward. It was likely written from Corinth in the spring of AD 57, before Paul delivered a collected offering to Jerusalem (15:23-28; Acts 20:2-3). It was also about three years into the reign of Nero, before his persecution of Christians began. The letter was apparently delivered by Phoebe (Romans 16:1-2; Cenchreae was Corinth's nearby port) and mentions at least two known residents of Corinth (Gaius and Erastus, 16:23). Though Corinth was a Greek city, the Corinthians prided themselves on their Roman-ness. It was an appropriate setting for writing this letter to the Romans.

Estimates of the number of Jews in Rome at the time range from ten thousand to fifty thousand, but they were still a small minority among the population of up to a million people. Just as there were several synagogues in the city, there were probably several house churches as well. Paul seems aware of at least four (16:5, 10-11, 15), and his letter is addressed to all of them (1:7).

Romans is widely considered Paul's most majestic, comprehensive letter, something resembling a systematic theology (or as close as Scripture ever comes to one), though he doesn't cover many key doctrines and seems focused more on accomplishing a specific purpose. But as we will see, the letter is not just a general statement of Christian beliefs. It's a personal letter to believers struggling with real issues and still learning the implications of believing in the God of Israel.

LIFE AS A ROMAN CHRISTIAN

Imagine being a Gentile believer in first-century Rome when your congregation receives a letter from Paul. Paul didn't plant your church—he had never been to the city at the time he wrote to you—but you've heard stories about its founding. The first members seem to have been Jews who embraced Jesus as the Messiah, and gradually God-fearing Gentiles like you, and other new converts, were drawn into the fellowship. In fact, that's how many churches throughout the Roman empire started. Yours just happens to be at the hub of the empire, and tens of thousands of Jews live there. It makes sense that they would be the first to receive this message.

A few years ago (AD 49), the emperor Claudius expelled Jews from the city over a controversy about "Chrestos," apparently Jesus. Not all Jews departed—logistics would have made such a large-scale exodus virtually impossible—but those involved in the controversy and many prominent leaders left, including many Jewish Christians. The church lost many of its founding members and leaders—Paul apparently ran into a couple of them in Corinth not long afterward (Acts 18:2)—and for a time, you wondered whether the Roman congregations would survive. They did, and some even thrived. Gentile believers who stepped into vacated leadership roles learned quickly. God brought your congregation through what had seemed like a devastating crisis at the time.

When Claudius died in AD 54, his edict expired with him, and Jews (and Jewish Christians) who had left Rome were allowed to return. Everyone in your church was relieved, but the return of the exiles created some unexpected issues. They had left as leaders, but those roles have now been filled by others. They had once been the majority, but with the addition of Gentile members, they are now a minority. You can sense the friction between genuine believers on both sides who are seeking the church's best interests but with competing claims to authority. This define-the-relationship season isn't easy on the fellowship.

Neither is the imperial culture. The verdict is still out on how Nero, the successor to Claudius, will treat Christians, but the imperial cult has been growing, and no one among your fellow believers can honestly affirm that "Caesar is Lord," as every Roman is expected to do. Hardly anyone beyond the churches and synagogues in the city—or in the rest of the empire, for that matter—can comprehend a religion that doesn't involve local temples, shrines, sacrifices, and other rituals, or even the idea that only one true God exists, and many people look down on you for honoring the God of those oddly countercultural Jews. Some who have learned of your beliefs wonder what this God requires of his worshipers and what he gives in return. Some think you're neglecting your civic responsibility and behaving very un-Roman-like. Even some of the newest believers in your church still wrestle with these issues.

To be honest, so do you. You aren't about to recant the faith that has so radically changed your life, but you wonder why so few people think the Good News is all that good—or even relevant. Many of your Roman compatriots consider it strange news, if they consider it at all, and your fellow believers who are Jewish seem disillusioned that so many of their people are now distancing themselves from the Jesus movement. If God's great salvation for his chosen people is rejected by most of them, have his age-old promises to them failed? Having longed for a messiah for centuries, have they taken a look at the one who has come to fulfill the promise and decided to give up hope instead? Has God rejected them now in favor of Gentiles? The Good News of salvation seems to have come with some very troubling consequences.

This reconstruction of the context in Rome at the time of Paul's writing requires some speculation, but not much. This is how historical events in the AD 50s would have shaped Christian experiences to some degree, and we see evidence of it in Paul's letter. He emphasizes Israel's faith and history but also assumes he is writing to a largely Gentile audience (see Romans 1:13; 11:13;

15:15-16). And reading between the lines of his argument, it isn't difficult to see the likelihood of Jewish and Gentile Christians sorting out their relationship and raising some serious concerns. The letter is sweeping in its theological scope, but also particular in showing two groups of believers their common ground. Romans wasn't written in a vacuum. Paul didn't just happen to be in the mood to lay out a grand vision of salvation. He addresses some thorny issues that were troubling the believers at a pivotal moment in history in the most influential city in the Mediterranean world.

PAUL'S PURPOSE IN WRITING

Because Paul had not yet been to Rome, he'd had no hand in establishing the city's churches. But Rome was the imperial heart, the power center of the world Paul lived in, and therefore a huge attraction for someone called to reach the world with the gospel. Unable to visit but hoping to pass through the city on an upcoming journey, he wrote this letter to share his intentions with the city's believers.

He also wrote to address some of the problems and concerns these churches were facing. There seems to have been tension between Jewish and Gentile factions, each group apparently misperceiving the other's role in God's purposes. Those misperceptions must have raised some difficult questions about Israel's place in the story of redemption; how the law (actually the whole Torah) applied to followers of Jesus, whether Jew or Gentile; whether there was still any point to being Jewish; why the majority of Jews were rejecting their own Messiah while many Gentiles with no background in God's long revelation received him so easily; and, in light of this perplexing turn of events, whether God was being faithful to his own promises that he had sworn to fulfill.

Paul addresses each of these questions while also offering an expansive view of redemption history and casting a stirring vision of the new humanity being birthed in Jesus and empowered by the Holy Spirit. The breadth of the letter has led various commentators to see it primarily as a presentation of the salvation message;* a theodicy, a "defense" of God's ways; Paul's version of a systematic theology; or a pastoral letter that, in addressing specific

* Martin Luther, John Calvin, and other Reformers (and countless Protestants thereafter).

beliefs and problems in the church, goes well beyond most in explaining foundational truths. Regardless of Paul's specific purpose, the result is multifaceted and far-reaching.

There is considerable debate about whether Jews of the first century thought they earned salvation by doing the works of the law (as was the assumption of the sixteenth-century Reformers), or that they did the works of the law because God had already saved them—that is, because God had chosen them and given them the law, they were obliged to live out that covenant. If the first assumption is true, Paul is writing about how all people, who are unrighteous, can be saved. If the second is true, Paul is writing about how God's works among the Jews now apply to all people, including Gentiles. Both views overgeneralize; presumably neither one fully captures Paul's thought, because it isn't possible to precisely reconstruct the situation in the Roman churches and the motives in Paul's heart. But elements of both views are found in his letter.

In any case, Paul's letters were always directed toward specific situations, even when the discussion broadened to the bigger picture. In Romans, the picture is as big as it gets. It is a vital letter for understanding the gospel message and even all of Scripture.

ROMANS AND US

Martin Luther thought that Romans and Galatians were the two most important letters in Scripture and recommended reading them once every week. He had his reasons; they addressed a very pressing concern in the early sixteenth century and shaped his foundational belief about justification by grace through faith alone. For that foundational premise, Romans is always relevant.

But we should never mistake Romans for a comprehensive presentation of New Testament theology. Nowhere in the letter does Paul address certain crucial doctrines: for example, the nature of Jesus as God and man, his return at the end of the age, or the doctrine of the church (other than its characteristics as one body). He gives a clear and powerful presentation of some—but not all—big-picture truths.

One of the best ways to grasp the meaning of a biblical book is to put yourself in the place of its original readers. The preceding exercise in imagining life as a Roman Christian gets us started, but we should maintain that perspective all the way through the letter, as much as modern believers can. Though based on God's promises to Israel, these words were written to Gentile and Jewish believers in a new and growing community of faith that had become available to all.

Throughout the letter, vital truths emerge, including humanity's universal predicament, the nature of the message of salvation by grace through faith, the relationship between faith and works, the death of our old life and the gift of new life through the resurrection of Jesus, how this all fits in God's overall plans, and what it all means for daily life. Read for the depth and details, but never lose sight of the breadth of the vision Paul presents.

These truths always apply, and we'll never exhaust the meaning and insights that come from them. They will always drive us deeper and make us stronger. See them all as invitations to experience the fullness of new life in ever-increasing wisdom, power, and love.

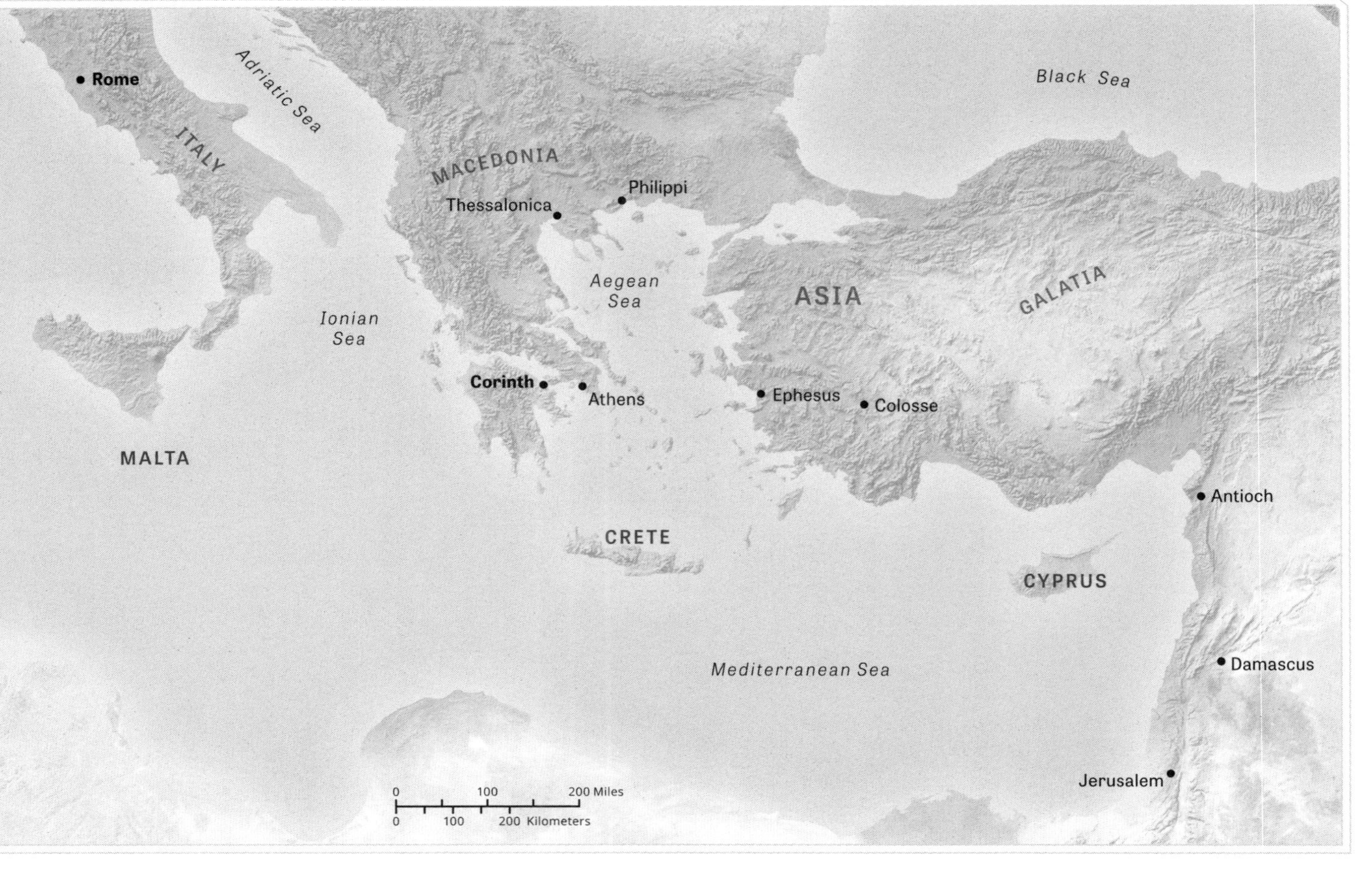
Rome
Adriatic Sea
ITALY
MALTA
Ionian Sea
MACEDONIA
Thessalonica
Philippi
Aegean Sea
Corinth
Athens
CRETE
ASIA
Ephesus
Colosse
GALATIA
Black Sea
Antioch
CYPRUS
Mediterranean Sea
Damascus
Jerusalem
0 100 200 Miles
0 100 200 Kilometers

THE UNIVERSAL PROBLEM

For an ancient letter, the beginning of Romans is fairly standard, and it doesn't take Paul long to dive into his purposes for writing. As he does, he builds a connection with the Christians in this city he has never seen. He addresses them as Gentiles—though there are Jewish believers among them—pointing out that this "Jewish" gospel is for all nations, including those represented in Rome. He is grateful for all the believers there and longs to visit them.

Because of apparent tensions and misunderstandings between Jews and Gentiles in the Roman churches, Paul wants to set the stage for what God is doing in the world in this age. The context for this gospel is the fact of desperate human need—spiritual depravity with its moral, social, and intellectual consequences. This need is shared by everyone, Jew and Gentile alike. No one has the upper hand. All are on level ground.

Perhaps Paul's words come across as general theology, but there's a more specific purpose behind them. (There always is.) The gospel only makes sense in this context, and heirs of the gospel can get along only when they understand how equally they need it. The rest of the letter depends on this setup. Without Jesus, everyone on earth—the people Paul is writing to and about, and also Paul himself—lives in foolishness and rebellion. With Jesus, everything becomes new.

BACKGROUND

In leveling the ground beneath the Jews and Gentiles, Paul deftly sides with both groups, even as he establishes the depravity of the entire human race. Jews were especially appalled by Gentile sexual perversion, licentiousness, and idolatry, which proliferated (often in connection with each other) in large cities like Rome. Paul joins in their revulsion (1:18-32). Gentiles were likewise turned off by Jewish pride in their heritage and chosenness, and Paul joins in their distaste for it (2:12-29). Read through the lens of each group's biases, these passages shed light on the dynamics between them. They also reveal the genius of Paul's rhetoric.

Which group was now favored by God? Apparently this was a point of contention, as Paul had likely heard. He had connections in Rome, including Priscilla and Aquila, whom he had met in Corinth (Acts 18:1-3, 18) and who now hosted a house church in Rome (Romans 16:3-5). They and other Jewish believers rightly understood the chosenness of their people. But Rome had gone from being a regional power to a vast and wealthy empire in less than three centuries. It seemed to be on the rise, and Jews seemed to be increasingly marginalized. If the Jewish gospel was being preached to Gentiles with greater results, did it mean that God's hand had shifted to the people most responsive to him?

As a Jew called to reach Gentiles, Paul was uniquely positioned to answer these kinds of questions, ease tensions, and help each group understand its ordained place in God's purposes. And even though he had no direct experience with the churches in Rome, he had longed to visit them. He must have seen this center of Gentile power, the capital city of his vision, as vital to his mission. The apostle to Gentiles could hardly have stayed away forever.

This is the context behind the opening to the letter. Paul begins by mentioning his own calling. Then he thoroughly establishes the roots of the gospel in Israel's history and Scriptures, but also affirms the inclusion of Gentiles (1:1-6)—incorporating several "counter-imperial signals" that point to Jesus, not Caesar, as the world's true Lord.* He will claim that a higher, greater kingdom than Rome is rising, which will carry more thorough and lasting salvation, peace, and justice—all benefits of the empire touted by Roman elites—but first he must establish our fallen, futile condition. He can hardly offer a picture of a new humanity until he has shown us the tragic predicament of the old—a predicament in which Jews and Gentiles share equally.

THE BIG PICTURE

In many ways, 1:16-17 states Paul's purpose in writing and gives us an outline of where he's headed. He will explain how God's righteousness is revealed (chapters 1–3), demonstrate God's power at work to save us through faith (chapters 4–11), and show us how to live by this faith (chapters 12–15). Over the course of the letter, we will see a gospel that transcends earthly empires (and emperors), racial and cultural barriers, and even sacred religious traditions. It also has the power to fundamentally alter the human condition. By receiving this salvation—this *rightness*—by faith, we become something we were not and enter into our original design, which we have not yet experienced.

In Paul's day, the false wisdom mentioned in 1:21-22 took the form of empty idolatry of statues and shrines. In ours, it's empty philosophy, secularism, and dependence on a finite and faulty intellect that together suggest the world could be self-created (therefore making us independent and not obligated to honor any higher being). This age-old darkness may look like light as new ideas develop, but it's the same old emptiness. The world insists that followers of Jesus are living in a fiction, as deluded people with an imaginary friend. Paul reveals how those in the world are the ones living in delusion, unaware of the horrific plight of all humanity.

This is why the promise of Romans—the fundamental transformation of human nature through the life and resurrection of the perfect Bearer of the image of God—is humanity's only hope. No law, philosophy, or earthly kingdom can change us. They can only expose our utter inability to overcome our fallenness. And that is exactly the message of this letter. Yes, we are trapped in our own futility, but our fallenness has been overcome in Jesus. An entirely new life—a new *kind* of life, in fact—unfolds for those who believe.

* N. T. Wright, *Paul: In Fresh Perspective* (Minneapolis: Fortress Press, 2005), 76.

EVERYONE EVERYWHERE

Through Christ, God has given us the privilege and authority as apostles to tell Gentiles everywhere what God has done for them.

1:5

Imagine people outside the church, even from distinctly non-Christian cultures, surprisingly becoming Christians. Most of us would be thrilled by this demonstration of God's power and grace. But what if, because of their radical conversion experience, they began teaching longtime churchgoers about Jesus and the power of the Holy Spirit—all while defying some of our treasured, traditional definitions of godliness? We can assume that some branches of the church would welcome them while resenting their quick assumptions of leadership roles, some would be highly suspicious of them for not following familiar paths into the faith, and some might even call them false teachers. New movements and trends always draw a range of responses among believers.

In some respects, this is just human nature. If something or someone doesn't align with our long-held assumptions and fit our humanly defined orthodoxy, we are reluctant to support it. Yet God has a track record of working in surprising ways. We tend to forget how surprising it was for God incarnate to come as a baby in a manger, offer life through a humiliating execution, and use the foolish things of this world to shame the wise.

We don't have to imagine the scenario described above. Something like it is happening in many parts of the world today as God brings "unlikely" believers into his Kingdom. That was the experience of the early church as well. God was reaching across ethnic and religious divides to draw many to himself. Paul saw it as his mission to proclaim this message to "Gentiles everywhere"—literally "all nations." A salvation rooted in Israel's history (1:2-4) was now open to everyone. Jesus was being presented as the rightful Lord of everyone the Roman empire ruled. And this transition from a "Jewish gospel" to an "everybody gospel" had become rather controversial.

RE-ENVISION THE "OTHERS"

It's natural to see the world around us in terms of "us" and "them." Virtually everyone does—religiously, politically, socially, ethnically, economically, and more. But the gospel breaks down old categories of "us" and "them" and insists that everyone who is "them" is a candidate to become "us." It's a reminder to expect the unexpected with God.

Do everything you can to maintain your vision of the God who defies assumptions and goes to extravagant lengths to reach the world—even in ways that might seem uncomfortable to his people. Practice seeing "them" as "us" and pray with all your heart for God to break down every barrier to his love and mercy—including any that may linger within your own heart.

THE GIFT EXCHANGE

I long to visit you so I can bring you some spiritual gift that will help you grow strong in the Lord.

1:11

We can't give others our own talents, instincts, or experiences. They are unique to us and nontransferable. But apparently we can impart spiritual gifts to each other. Paul planned to do exactly that when he visited the Romans. It was one of his reasons for wanting to go there.

What kind of gift does Paul have in mind here? Is it the kind he lists in other places (such as Romans 12 or 1 Corinthians 12), which empower people to fulfill some specific spiritual assignment? Or is it a broader gift or blessing—such as faith, inspiration, or wisdom? His choice of words seems to imply the sort of gift he itemizes elsewhere, and that he can stir up or impart those gifts by fellowshipping with and praying for the Romans. He seems to catch himself mid-sentence to recognize the reciprocity of it all—that he might be encouraged by them too (1:12). But his focus is on giving them something of what God has given him.

In any case, this idea might be a little surprising to those in an individualistic culture like ours that emphasizes a one-to-one relationship with the Holy Spirit and receiving things directly from him. But spiritual gifts in the New Testament imply some degree of interaction. Everyone involved in exercising them needs each other. Just as we can't experience the range of God's creativity by gazing at one mountain or ocean, we can't experience the fullness of his power and grace by limiting our fellowship. We are part of a whole.

RE-ENVISION SPIRITUAL CONNECTIONS

Interdependence is highly valued in the Kingdom of God. It's part of the culture. We can't get everything we need from God without other people, and others can't get everything they need from him without us. Yes, there's unusual grace for people who persist in their faith in isolation, like prisoners or the socially marginalized, but under normal circumstances, being connected with other believers is vital for our spiritual growth and encounters with God.

Paul will expand on this later when he describes the nature of spiritual gifts and insists that "we all belong to each other" (12:5), because that picture of spiritual union is important. We have to see ourselves as members who impart spiritual gifts, blessings, and truths to each other and eagerly receive them from one another if we are going to experience God as fully as he wants us to. Every Christian gathering is in some sense a gift exchange, and we all benefit.

UNASHAMED

I am not ashamed of this Good News about Christ. It is the power of God at work, saving everyone who believes—the Jew first and also the Gentile.

1:16

Hardly any Christian would admit to being ashamed of the gospel, yet many keep it under wraps because of the reactions it can provoke. But not Paul. Using language and concepts that echo (and implicitly mock) imperial claims—power, justice, loyalty, salvation—Paul boldly claims the superiority of the gospel message over anything the world has to offer. He shows us what it looks like to have more confidence in God's power to work through the gospel than in our culture's power to quench it. He is far more concerned about advancing the Kingdom than guarding his own reputation.

What does Paul mean that the gospel is the power of God for salvation? The gospel isn't just a message, a philosophy, or a principle to agree with. It's the powerful agent of redemption, renewal, and restoration for our world. For centuries, philosophers and sages have carried on endless debates in their search for truth and meaning—and yet *we* have the answer. Most of these theorists would reject it because it ends the debate (which they love) and doesn't fit many of their cherished assumptions, but it's still the truth. And it's the only truth with the power to bring lasting—even eternal—transformation to people's lives. It's our only link to the new creation God is bringing about. It's the lifeline for a dying world. As much as people may try to shame us for our beliefs, there's nothing to be ashamed of in the gospel.

RE-ENVISION YOUR MESSAGE

In the eyes of many Christians, the Good News about Jesus is cowering in the corner of our culture while the world's ideas seem bigger and more powerful simply because they're more popular. We need to dispel this distorted vision. We also have to be less concerned about our reputation and willing to take some hits for what we believe. As Paul will remind us, no pain or discomfort now can compare to the glory we will experience later.

Focusing on long-term gains instead of short-term costs is the difference between living with a big vision and living with a small one. People around you will notice the message you're living, whether you want them to or not. Live and speak as though the gospel is the greatest power in the world—because it is. The more fully you embrace that vision, the more clearly the world will see it.

This Good News tells us how God makes us right in his sight. This is accomplished from start to finish by faith. As the Scriptures say, "It is through faith that a righteous person has life."

1:17

Paul quotes Habakkuk 2:4 here and in Galatians 3:11. Familiarly translated "The just shall live by faith," it became the theological centerpiece for Martin Luther and other sixteenth-century Reformers. The statement can legitimately be read several ways:

- "The righteous will live a lifestyle of faith,"
- "Living by faith makes us righteous," or
- "By faith, the righteous obtain life."

The third meaning is the one that became so central to the Reformation, and to Protestant theology thereafter, but all are true. And as we can see from the repetition—words for "faith" and "believe" are used four times in the original language of verses 16-17—*faith* is the central attribute of the Christian life.

In fact, faith is central to God's Kingdom as a whole. Without faith, we can't get anything that lasts. It's the currency by which we receive salvation, answers to prayer, spiritual growth, our awareness of God's presence, and our experience of his Spirit's power. This is how we advance the Kingdom on earth. It's the foundational operating principle for God's people.

With faith at the center of our lives, we recognize that mere human effort does not accomplish anything eternal. Our belief in what God has done does. Verse 17 tells us that God's righteousness is revealed in this gospel. We believe in his righteousness, not our own, and with that faith receive life and walk in his power. Our entire lives depend on it.

RE-ENVISION FAITH

Learn to see the power of faith not as a faint hope but as a mountain-moving, sea-changing, life-transforming force. It transcends human reasoning and circumstances. When you invite God into a situation, faith transcends any earthly obstacle you might face. Without it, you can't grow spiritually, pray for someone effectively, or even experience new life. With it, nothing is impossible. At times you may feel wildly presumptuous in having the faith God wants you to have—Scripture is full of examples—but you can't please him without it (Hebrews 11:6). Like the Reformers, make faith the substance of your salvation—and every aspect of living it out.

GOD MADE VISIBLE

Through everything God made, they can clearly see his invisible qualities—his eternal power and divine nature. So they have no excuse for not knowing God.

1:20

A good Jew like Paul would surely emphasize that God can be known through Torah—the Hebrew Scriptures. So pointing to creation as a revelation of God reminds us of his largely Gentile audience for this letter (see also 1:6). He'll address the Jews later—the first few chapters of Romans cover the entire human race—but for now, he wants Gentile believers to remember where they came from. The vast numbers of Gentiles who have never read Torah and do not know Jesus should at least know something about the true God.

Many people would have thought that God had only revealed himself through his covenant people and the Word he gave them. Not so, says Paul. His invisible attributes can be known through the visible world. Those who don't see them have chosen to ignore the evidence.

In the last half of Romans 1, Paul paints a picture of the world as broken and living in rebellion, whether consciously or not. It's easy to condemn these people—Paul certainly condemns their choices—but that isn't his main purpose. He is setting up the solution by focusing on the problem. We live in a world in desperate need of this powerful gospel. People who are ignorant of God through their own choices may act like our enemies, but they are precious to God. They may have keen intellects, but their worldview is woefully insufficient and distorted. They are hungry for the very truth they keep at arm's length.

"They" are the focus of this passage—Paul will turn to "we" soon enough—but this picture hit close to home for many of this letter's first readers who had come out of a pagan background. They were the exceptions in responding to the gospel message. Yes, there are people who have never heard of Jesus through no fault of their own, but there comes a point in every person's life when he or she encounters some evidence or attribute of God and then faces a choice: whether to pursue more or brush it off. Paul says that the people who don't know God chose in that moment (or many moments) to brush him off. The Roman believers Paul is writing to did not.

RE-ENVISION REVELATION

As a believer, you know God through the direct revelation of Scripture. But it's also important to learn to see him in *everything*. Don't just observe an ocean or a starry sky; see God's vastness. Don't just marvel at the intricacies of the human body; notice God's brilliant design. Don't just see a positive or negative circumstance as a good or bad turn of events; see God's sovereign hand (and if that turn of events is bad, perhaps see also an invitation to engage in battle to advance his Kingdom). God is revealing himself to believers and nonbelievers alike all the time. Open your eyes and ask for the vision to see him everywhere.

DESCENT INTO DARKNESS

They knew God, but they wouldn't worship him as God or even give him thanks. . . . Their minds became dark and confused. Claiming to be wise, they instead became utter fools. And instead of worshiping the glorious, ever-living God, they worshiped idols.

1:21-23

Passages like this may give the impression that all ancient Greeks and Romans worshiped at the shrines of idols and engaged in reckless promiscuity (perhaps even at those same shrines). But many people in Paul's day were a lot like most people today. They worked hard, loved their families, practiced culturally accepted religion (which generally didn't focus on ethics and morals), and embraced various philosophies (which *did* focus on ethics and morals). It was a very diverse world, with the kinds of extreme degradation described here and the kind of normalcy most of us would find familiar. Still, from one end of the spectrum to the other, according to Paul, no one has an excuse for not knowing the true God.

What began this downward spiral into utter depravity? Recognizing God without worshiping or thanking him. There's a connection between ingratitude and a darkened understanding (which also suggests a connection between gratitude and enlightened understanding). Worship and gratitude keep us aware of who God is, what he is like, and what he does. Otherwise, we search for meaning and purpose with compromised understanding, eventually claiming wisdom but remaining fools. Paul is simply observing that humanity has lost its true vision and replaced it with false visions. Once we've become unanchored to truth, we dream dreams that aren't from God, make plans that don't fit his purposes, and pursue agendas that contradict his Kingdom in favor of our own. We live in our own fiction.

RE-ENVISION THE POWER OF GRATITUDE

Worshipful gratitude is not just a polite response to receiving God's gifts. It's a powerful, situation-changing attitude. We need a restored vision of how gratitude can change the course of our lives and the lives of people around us.

A life of honoring God brings increasing wisdom, revelation, guidance, and divine intervention. A life of not honoring him obscures everything. He acknowledges that choice and lets people go their own way, and they begin to live in a self-made fantasy that can seem very true. Science fiction writers imagine life-altering realities that change everything we know. We have a true, life-altering reality in the gospel. Awaken to it. Saturate yourself in worshipful gratitude and you'll see it. It's a clear contrast to worldly wisdom—and powerful evidence that you are anchored in truth.

They traded the truth about God for a lie. So they worshiped and served the things God created instead of the Creator himself, who is worthy of eternal praise! Amen. That is why God abandoned them to their shameful desires. . . . Their lives became full of every kind of wickedness.

1:25-26, 29

There are serious consequences to brushing off God. Once the true God becomes obscure to us, we descend into darkness. Hearts grow dull, minds come up with all kinds of rationales for their own constructs, vision fades or gets diverted toward less worthy pursuits, and we end up asking, *What is the meaning of it all? Is there any point?*

In the exchanges made by sinful hearts—truth for lies, the Creator for the created, God-given desires for shameful desires, the natural for the unnatural—meaning and purpose are hard to see. The convoluted rationales of Paul's day and ours call lies *truth*, the created *glorious*, distorted passions *normal*, and the unnatural *natural*. It's no wonder, in all these radical redefinitions, that our worship, beliefs, and practices look strange and distorted to the unbelieving world. We have a completely different frame of reference.

Throughout this passage, Paul refers to some sexual practices that were widely accepted in the Greek and Roman world—and may not have been a big deal to some of his readers, even after they had accepted Christ. They had grown up in that context. They no longer agreed with this kind of immorality, but they weren't shocked by it. They had to learn to see truth, ethics, and morality in new ways.

RE-ENVISION THE WORLD

We need to see the world in new ways. Human thought is not just a matter of diverse viewpoints but of truth and lies, of the Creator's original design and humanity's distortion of it. We are in no position to condemn the world for this; we participated in this distortion, and we likely carry remnants of it with us. But we do have to see the problem. Otherwise we'll conform to "choices" rather than reality.

This part of Paul's letter is not very encouraging—the encouragement comes later—but in envisioning the world's darkness, he also envisions hope. Remember the idea that undergirds this section: *the power of the gospel to save* (1:16). In fact, the rest of the letter boldly and triumphantly presents God's solution. Above all, fill your vision with that. Make it your mission to see and live the truth in a darkened world that desperately needs it.

A SHARED BROKENNESS

Since you judge others for doing these things, why do you think you can avoid God's judgment when you do the same things?

2:3

Paul has exposed the pagan world's sinfulness, and even Rome's recent Gentile converts to the faith would likely have agreed with his assessment and judged people accordingly. Many of their friends and acquaintances were full participants in the decay of humanity. They were blind to the truth.

But now, in Paul's rhetorical turn, "they" becomes "you." These Gentile believers (and every one of us as well) are part of the problem—especially any who have brought pagan values and ideas into their new life. No, these Roman Christians (one would hope) haven't been worshiping at shrines, engaging in sexual perversion, or acting like fools as they profess their own wisdom. Human depravity isn't quite so obvious in most people's lives. But they (and we) have all come out of the same rebellion and participated in it to one degree or another. We may have failed God's standards by different degrees, but we've all failed. We can't claim the moral high ground. Instead of directing judgment at others, we have to see ourselves, in our original state, as thoroughly needy before God.

RE-ENVISION YOUR CONDITION

We love to envision separation between ourselves and the unbelieving world, and our salvation does create a separation. But we also must remember our need. There was something fundamentally flawed in all of us. Deep down inside, we were broken and insecure, always compensating, constructing false "truths" and our own sense of significance so we wouldn't have to admit the painful truth about ourselves. Some of us are still doing that.

A vision of this universal need eliminates judgment, doesn't it? Not the kind of judgment that discerns right and wrong, which is necessary, but we can no longer point the finger as if we're from better stock than the sinful people Paul describes. When we acknowledge that *we* were dead in our sin (Ephesians 2:1), prisoners of a fallen creation, we can have nothing but gratitude for being raised to new life. Hearts full of thankfulness have little room to judge people in the same condition we came from.

Be careful with this vision, though. It's important to see your sinful, broken condition as your *past*, not your present. That fact alone is enough to keep you from self-righteousness. It's even more important to see yourself as a new creation with a new heart and a new nature, even when you see contrary evidence in your own thoughts and behaviors. In fact, Paul will insist on this new vision of yourself in chapter 6. Know your brokenness, but live in your healing. This powerful gospel transforms you completely.

TRANSFORMING KINDNESS

Don't you see how wonderfully kind, tolerant, and patient God is with you? Does this mean nothing to you? Can't you see that his kindness is intended to turn you from your sin?

2:4

We all see God through a certain lens, and that lens is colored by many factors. Some see him as a taskmaster, others as a detached observer, and still others as a heavenly vending machine, the God of truth but not love, the God of love but not truth, or the God whose arm we have to twist to get anything. We usually aren't aware of these assumptions, but they're there. Parent figures, our experiences, and our internal biases have shaped them. And they all give us a distorted picture of God.

To be fair, no one sees God completely clearly, because we are finite and flawed and he is infinite and perfect. We can't comprehend his full range of attributes. People in Scripture who saw him were overwhelmed, speechless, terrified, or stupefied. Like household wiring blown by a massive electric surge, we don't have the capacity to fully grasp him.

But we don't have to see God fully to know him accurately. Having labeled the entire Gentile world as depraved, Paul presents God as kind, tolerant, and patient—and tells us to view him through a lens of kindness that assumes his goodwill. In every situation, we can know that he is doing something good and is favorably disposed toward us. That's his nature.

Our religious instincts tell us that God's wrath provokes repentance, but Paul says it's his kindness instead. He means to draw us toward himself by showing us how good he is. Those who see him through the wrong lens miss that message, but sensitive, open hearts will not. His true nature, if we can see it, stirs up our love.

RE-ENVISION GOD

When we view God as a hard master, an overindulgent parent, a means to get what we want, an absentee landlord, or some other distortion of his nature, we will always misinterpret his gifts, his patience, and our circumstances. But the eyes of faith repent of false images, recognize God's kindness, and wonder: *What if my greatest disappointments are really evidence of his great protection? What if I've been pleading to a God who has already said yes and is simply waiting for me to believe? What if his most extravagant promises in Scripture are . . . for me?* These are thoughts that empower us to know him, experience him, and step into his fullness.

He will judge everyone according to what they have done.

2:6

Romans and Galatians have long been heralded by Protestants as the letters that most clearly present the gospel of salvation by grace through faith alone. These are also the two letters in which Paul quotes Habakkuk 2:4: "The just shall live by his faith" (NKJV). Yet here in the text of Romans, Paul makes a statement that seems completely contrary to his own beliefs: "He [God] will judge everyone according to what they have done."

There are at least three ways to interpret that statement: (1) as a description of our fate without Christ, as if we had nothing but our own insufficient righteousness to depend on; (2) as a reminder of punishment for the unsaved and rewards for the saved—the works we do that have eternal value (1 Corinthians 3:12-15); or (3) as the works that flow out of our faith as evidence that we truly believe (James 2:14-17)—the real issue being the faith that produces works, not the works themselves.

Paul has already described those who are outside of Christ. Here he is writing to Christians, and he has tied this statement about judgment to eternal life (Romans 2:7), leaving only the third interpretation as the one that makes sense. It reconciles salvation by grace through faith with God's emphasis on judgment and rewards (Psalm 62:12; Proverbs 24:12; Matthew 16:27; John 5:28-29;

2 Corinthians 5:10; 1 Peter 1:17). Many commentators have suggested that Paul and James are completely at odds, but here Paul is making a very Jamesian argument. His entire theology throughout all his letters hinges on being saved by grace through faith, not by works. We are made righteous by our faith. But those who have been made righteous will do righteous things.

RE-ENVISION YOUR WORKS

Do you see works as a means to your salvation, or as an add-on that may be important but isn't essential to your salvation? The truth is that both visions are flawed. Resist them and instead envision your entire life—beliefs, words, behaviors, and acts of service that flow from faith, worship, love, and gratitude—as all part of the same package. God never intended for us to be fractured, compartmentalized beings who believe one thing and yet live out another. His presence and power within us affect everything.

It is important to see yourself entirely outside of the works/judgment conundrum. Jesus has lifted us beyond it. But it is also important to see your works as an overflow of your relationship with Jesus. When the works aren't flowing, don't just try to do more. Instead, check the relationship. Trust Jesus to fill your life with passion for his presence, purposes, and power, and let his works flow through you.

OPEN BLESSINGS

God does not show favoritism.

2:11

The first eleven chapters of Genesis paint a picture of human history. But in chapter 12, the narrative turns to a specific man as the father of a specific people. Through Abraham and his descendants, all the world would be blessed. And from that point forward, Scripture refers to the Hebrew people as God's chosen.

Does that mean God plays favorites? After all, as Paul points out, God said through Malachi that he loved Jacob and rejected Esau and will show compassion to whomever he chooses (Romans 9:13-14, quoting Malachi 1:2-3). Yet he makes those choices according to his divine purposes, not according to our merit. God called Israel his firstborn (Exodus 4:22), implying there would be later-born people as well. In an age in which God had thrown open the doors of salvation to all who believe, he clearly demonstrated that Israel's later-born siblings among the Gentiles were welcomed into the family.

God's lack of favoritism in the context of Paul's argument means he applies his judgment evenly (Romans 2:7-11)—to Gentiles and Jews, believers and nonbelievers, according to universal standards. Peter marveled at God's impartiality when he realized God had arranged for him to preach to uncircumcised Gentile believers (Acts 10:34-35). Throughout the New Testament, the message is that God's favor for Israel is available to all people groups. As a broader principle, we can assume it applies to all people individually too.

Does that mean God blesses everyone equally? Not at all. He favors those who know who he is and believe accordingly—who stake their lives on his kindness (Romans 2:4). Negative people receive grace, but they don't do great works of faith or experience great overflows of God's favor. People who believe boldly do. He is partial to them. But the invitation to become the kind of person he blesses is available to all without partiality. He is not seeking people with a long Jewish or Christian heritage, spiritual insiders, or the religiously approved. Yesterday's unlikely convert can be today's world-changing believer.

RE-ENVISION FAVOR

Refuse any assumption or perception that God blesses other people more than he blesses you. You may have seen some evidence for that—we all do at times—but it's not because of who you are. It's because something—some belief, assumption, perception, or lie—is interfering with your faith. Find your identity fully in him, believe what the New Testament says about you, and step into the fullness of his blessing. Like everyone else who loves God wholeheartedly, you'll find his favor there.

LAWS OF THE HEART

They demonstrate that God's law is written in their hearts, for their own conscience and thoughts either accuse them or tell them they are doing right.

2:15

A Gentile convert in Rome probably would have been quite relieved not to have to learn all the details of the Jewish law and live up to them. Gentile believers had received salvation by grace through faith, bypassing all the legalities and ritualism. Many were learning the amazing story of God's work through Israel, and all would certainly accept the morality of the Ten Commandments, but few were interested in Israel's Levitical laws and traditions. Salvation by grace was much simpler and far more liberating.

Imagine their surprise, then, when Paul begins talking about the law in a way that includes Gentiles' failure to live up to it. Ignorance of the law is not an excuse because everyone has a conscience, and everyone has failed to live up to what their conscience tells them. We each have an instinctive law placed within us—not in Torah-level detail but with a basic, universal sense of what is right and wrong—and still we've all failed. According to 2:12, not knowing the law is not a good excuse for Gentiles, and knowing the law isn't enough for Jews. All have fallen short in their own way.

As born-again believers, our instinctive conscience has now been shaped and inspired by the Holy Spirit within us. We hear his inner voice. Many people aren't so sure, but only because they have trouble distinguishing his voice from myriad others, not because he isn't speaking. He is at work within us so we can discern, desire, and display his purposes (Philippians 2:13). Our inner compass has become his mouthpiece.

RE-ENVISION YOUR COMPASS

Picture your conscience as a holy compass—something like a wind sock indicating the direction of the Holy Spirit's breath. According to Jesus and the New Testament writers, the Spirit is present within you and eager to fill you with truth and character. Yes, you've defied your conscience before, both before and after you were born of the Spirit. We all have. But the invitation remains to let yourself be moved by him in all ways (John 3:8). The Christian life is not so much a matter of living up to a standard as it is a matter of eliminating resistance to God's presence and power within us. Not only does he call us into truth; he also fills us with his life to live it out.

HYPOCRISY'S TESTIMONY

No wonder the Scriptures say, "The Gentiles blaspheme the name of God because of you."

2:24

Paul has been addressing Gentiles, but Jews are listening too. Now he turns to them. And his words put both groups in the same position—as those who have fallen short of God's character.

If there was friction between Jews and Gentiles in the Roman churches, we can see how Paul's words would address those tensions. His reminders of pagan culture and a depraved background would soften the agendas of Gentiles jockeying to maintain their leadership roles after exiled Jewish leaders returned to the city. And his reminders of Israel's emphatic failures to live up to God's law would soften the attitudes of Jewish leaders depending on their pedigree as God's chosen people. Neither group could claim superiority in God's purposes. All were equally in need of grace.

In leveling the field, Paul points out the damage of an inconsistent testimony. If people don't live out what they profess to believe, their words become empty, and their lifestyle opens up their beliefs to ridicule. (Notice the reaction anytime a Christian leader today is accused of sexual or financial impropriety.) It's completely illogical to reject an entire belief system because some adherents are hypocrites, but that's the dynamic at work in the watching world. Jews claimed a special relationship with God marked by his righteousness—now

Christians do too—and Paul says they dishonored that relationship by claiming one thing and living another. Paul would know from his own experience that this testimony does enormous harm, and it can all be avoided with an attitude of true humility.

RE-ENVISION YOUR IMAGE

Scripture gives us glowing pictures of ourselves: beloved children of God, saints, new creations, God's workmanship, a royal priesthood, and many more. And they are all true. Embrace them fully. But they are never a basis for pride. Even amid the extravagant abundance of God's blessings, it's essential to see yourself as a humble recipient of grace and relate to others from that identity.

Those who claim righteousness and fall short of it are called hypocrites and are ridiculed for their terrible testimony. But humble recipients of grace never claim righteousness for themselves to begin with. Falling short of it fits the profile. If you never assume you're better than anyone, you can live in the freedom of a true self-perception—completely unpretentious, relying on the vast grace of God as a visible testimony for all who need it. Be genuine in your own insufficiency, exude the joy of someone whose God has overcome it, and let the world see what radical grace looks like.

CHANGE WITHIN

A true Jew is one whose heart is right with God. And true circumcision is not merely obeying the letter of the law; rather, it is a change of heart produced by the Spirit.

2:29

Paul had once taken pride in his background. In his testimony, repeated in Acts and his letters, he often mentioned his Jewish pedigree and Pharisaic training. He was thoroughly grounded in the history of his people. So when he wrote of those who relied on the law and boasted about their relationship with God (2:17), he wasn't only addressing the inflated pride of his compatriots. He was also pointing a finger at his former self.

That a zealous Jew would redefine Jewishness after meeting the Jewish Messiah is a spectacular testimony to the radical nature of Paul's experience. He never denied his Jewish identity, of course; as a believer in Jesus, he continued to observe Sabbaths, visit synagogues, and perform Temple rituals (Acts 21:17-26). But he did deny the value of that identity in reconciling a person to God (Philippians 3:3-11). He insisted that believing Gentiles, ill-trained in Jewish law and culture, were just as saved as he was.

So Paul separates the heart of Jewishness from its trappings. True circumcision is not a physical ritual but a spiritual consecration and inward transformation. The letter of the law is no longer the issue; it could never save a person anyway. The spirit of the law—or the law of the Spirit—is what matters. Righteousness is still tremendously important, but the law is not (nor ever has been) the way to attain it. It only reveals the need for salvation (Romans 3:20). We are both justified and transformed by faith.

RE-ENVISION THE GOAL

How we see our justification and transformation is vital. Salvation by grace through faith isn't about lowering our standards or redefining righteousness. It actually raises the standard—from our human ability to keep the law to God's ability to work his nature and character into us. If we are trying to manage sin, be as good as we can be (within reasonable expectations), and trust that God will cover our failures, we may have good intentions, but we are living the old, futile life.

We can live an entirely new life because we have become new creations, participants in the divine nature, temples of the Holy Spirit. This is an extraordinary vision of what human beings can become by faith and in God's power. Never define salvation simply as your entrance into the Kingdom. Salvation *is* the Kingdom. Believe that God is righteous within you, trust in the Spirit's presence and power, and let every area of your life be transformed.

THE PROMISE KEEPER

What's the advantage of being a Jew? . . . First of all, the Jews were entrusted with the whole revelation of God. True, some of them were unfaithful; but just because they were unfaithful, does that mean God will be unfaithful? Of course not! Even if everyone else is a liar, God is true.

3:1-4

Uniqueness was part of the Jewish identity. First-century Jews could not conceive of being anything other than chosen, beloved, and specially treasured by God in a unique relationship with him that other nations did not share. They would have known of certain Gentiles grafted into God's people—Rahab and Ruth, for two prominent examples—but the idea of being chosen and distinct was part of the Jews' identity. Paul's ministry to Gentiles was highly controversial because he seemed to be undermining that identity.

Paul doesn't shy away from that controversy in Romans. In fact, he leans into it. He essentially ascribes to Gentiles the same standing before God as those who had long considered themselves under God's covenant, kept his laws as well as they could, observed feasts and Temple sacrifices, clung to his promises, and valued their heritage as his people. How could all that not matter anymore? How could these latecomers from pagan backgrounds share in God's promises to his people? It didn't seem fair.

Still, Jews had certain advantages—not in receiving salvation but in stewarding its unfolding message. They had been entrusted with the story that created the context for everything God was doing in history. Through them, he demonstrated his love, power, righteousness, justice, grace, deliverance, healing, patience, kindness, and so much more. They were his vessels of revelation.

The fact that some were unfaithful says nothing about God's character, just as misguided professing Christians throughout the last two millennia—crusaders, colonizers, enslavers—say nothing about the message of Jesus (even when people use such abuses to castigate Christians). The question isn't whether people have deviated from God's goodness. It's whether God has remained faithful to it. And he has.

RE-ENVISION GOD'S FAITHFULNESS

For people who have been saved by grace through faith, we can be awfully focused on our own failures. Many of us become consumed with sins we've committed rather than the grace that has covered them. We live in guilt and shame rather than gratitude and freedom. That has to change.

Human history tells a story of futility. The long history of redemption through Israel and its Messiah tells a story of a new, unfettered destiny into a transcendent Kingdom of glory. God has faithfully brought you into it. When it really sinks in that his promise is true and not contingent on your goodness, guilt and shame dissolve and joy comes in. Turn your gaze from your own futility to the Promise Keeper who has made all things—including you—new.

THE LIBERTINE FALLACY

Some people even slander us by claiming that we say, "The more we sin, the better it is!" Those who say such things deserve to be condemned.

3:8

Apparently, rumors were swirling. Some who had grasped how radical Paul's message was—that living by grace through faith alone frees us from any penalty for sin—could see the implications. In theory, people could just keep on sinning and trust that their wrongdoing would further highlight God's righteousness. It's an easily exploited message. If it really is the truth—if everything depends on Jesus' righteous perfection and not ours—we have a license to sin, and he no longer has any basis to condemn us.

Paul will respond rather vehemently to this libertine idea again in 6:1-2, but he addresses it here in the context of God's justice and humanity's universal corruption. As a Pharisee, he must have had difficulty writing about God and unfairness in the same sentence (3:5). Nothing God does is unjust, and Paul goes out of his way to say that raising the possibility is just a rhetorical device. Yes, our sin demonstrates God's righteousness; and yes, his forgiveness demonstrates his mercy. But the suggestion that we might sin more to highlight God's righteousness more is a horrifying idea to someone preaching a salvation of righteousness by grace through faith. The argument misses the point completely.

We learn from this passage and 6:1-2 that Paul recognized how radical (and exploitable) his message was. On God's own terms of salvation by grace through faith in Jesus, we *technically* do have freedom to live without regard to righteousness. All things are now lawful, if not beneficial (1 Corinthians 10:23). But asking whether something is lawful or not is beside the point. With the Spirit powerfully at work within us, lawfulness is irrelevant. He is producing righteousness within us because we let him, and we let him because he has put within us the desire to become like he is. Our spiritual transformation sets sin—as well as libertinism and legalism—aside.

RE-ENVISION YOUR FREEDOM

If you're like most modern Christians who are serious about their salvation and all its implications, you may have embraced a "gospel of freedom" that still leaves you struggling to become righteous. Like many, you may have said, "The gospel doesn't free us to do what we want; it frees us to do what God wants." Yet doing what God wants still proves troublesome.

Any effort to follow an outward standard without inner transformation is a kind of law, an old-nature attempt to produce a new nature, and it always eventually fails. Stop trying. Instead, see your struggles as cues to invite the Holy Spirit into the process. Immerse yourself in the transformation he provides. Don't worry about temporary failures. The more you see yourself as new, the more you will live from your new nature, and the freer you will become to be who he made you to be.

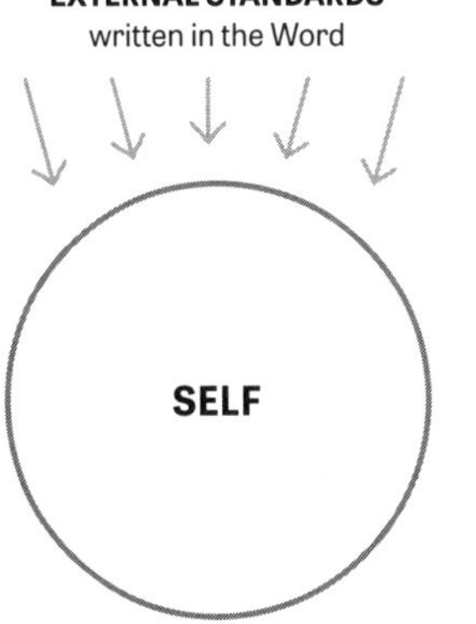

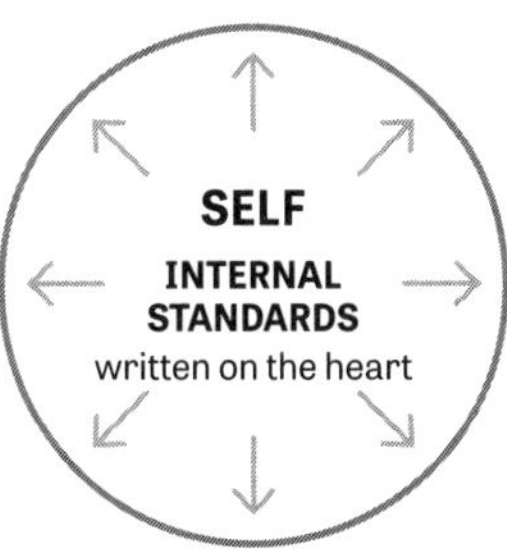

When we perceive standards as external instructions—whether they be God's laws and principles or our own conscience and morals—we either try to discipline ourselves to obey them (legalism) or seek freedom from them by denying them (lawlessness). Neither approach leads to real freedom. Throughout much of Romans, Paul will reveal how truth transforms us through the power of the Spirit as God plants his own nature within us. We are no longer constrained by law, but also no longer lawless and dangerous in our freedom. We are free to live according to our new nature, with truth written on our hearts in fulfillment of Old Testament prophecies (see Jeremiah 24:7; Ezekiel 11:19; 36:26-27).

A BROKEN POWER

All people, whether Jews or Gentiles, are under the power of sin. As the Scriptures say, "No one is righteous—not even one."

3:9-10

There's quite a contrast between the "great benefits" of being a Jew in 3:1-2 and their being "not at all" better than others in 3:9-10. But it isn't a contradiction. The Jewish experience was extremely valuable, not in getting people closer to God but in giving them understanding of his work in human history. They got to see it all unfold, even though they were equally in need of the salvation he brought about. No one, neither Jew nor Gentile, is righteous before God.

Paul demonstrates this universal sinfulness with rapid-fire, fragmented quotes from Hebrew Scripture (3:10-18) to prove that Jews are included in it. Perhaps it was a pressing question in Paul's day, at least among those with Jewish heritage, but we might wonder how relevant it is today. Most people in our generation aren't full of angst over their inability to be righteous. Most try to be decent people and let it go at that, because we're "all in the same boat," "only human," or consider ourselves inherently good from the start. When we present the gospel as a matter of being justified before God, a postmodern society yawns and says, "So what?"

But everyone experiences the frustration of living in a fallen world, even if most have resigned themselves to being stuck in it. Past generations wondered, *Is this all there is?* Many in this generation answer, *Yes*. But the gospel is not only about justification before God, as Paul will go on to explain. It's about a new creation that transcends this world that was once consigned to futility (8:20). By receiving salvation by grace through faith in Jesus, we aren't just given a new status before God. We enter into a thoroughly different reality.

RE-ENVISION REALITY

Science fiction enthusiasts love the idea of an alternate reality, some illusion-busting moment that offers a glimpse beyond the deceptive, confining mirage of life in this world—like the blue-pill, red-pill scene in the movie *The Matrix*, for example. We instinctively know there's more out there, some transcendent world beyond our vision. The gospel message of the New Testament opens our eyes to see it.

Stir up that vision of a new reality and immerse yourself in it. We are no longer "under the power of sin"—or of frustration, futility, meaninglessness, guilt, shame, brokenness, pain, or even death. The message of salvation by grace through faith isn't just about self-improvement, doing better, or even being rescued from our fallenness. It's about having been trapped in this world where sin, rebellion, and futility reign, with no apparent way out, and then being transferred into an existence in which no condition can enslave us. Like every human being, you've been well-trained in the experience of fallenness. Let go of that illusion, envision the promises of newness God has given you, and live in them freely.

THE END OF FUTILITY

No one can ever be made right with God by doing what the law commands. The law simply shows us how sinful we are.

3:20

The first three chapters of Romans raise some pretty big questions. One is how God can judge people who have never heard of him. Paul's answer is that anyone can know God simply by being observant and responding positively to what they can see around them (1:19-23). Another question is that if faithful Jews who have done their best to keep all the commandments and stay true to the covenant still aren't saved, isn't God being unfaithful to his own promises? If the efforts of past generations to follow him were destined to end in failure, wasn't God unfair to lead them on?

Paul's answer to the second question is that God has always made people righteous by faith alone—Abraham being the prime example—and Jews have always been able to believe in the means of their salvation, even before it was fully revealed in Jesus. But now that Jesus has come, Jews are obligated to respond to him just as Gentiles are. Righteousness by faith was always the plan, and now the plan is on display in Christ.

The biggest question, of course, is what it means to be made righteous. Is it simply being made legally and positionally right with God, or does it also include practical life change? Theologians debate such nuances, and Paul will address them in the next few chapters, but we already know God's desire: *that we be conformed to his image*. Salvation that doesn't dramatically move us in that direction would fall short of his design for us. We are to be made right—and righteous—in every way.

RE-ENVISION CHANGE

Human beings have tried many approaches to changing themselves, but always with limited success. Fallen flesh in a fallen world cannot overcome its own fallenness. People may reform their thoughts and behavior significantly, but genuine, self-generated transformation remains elusive.

But a Holy Spirit–inspired vision of who we really are in Christ changes everything. The law has shown us how sinful we are; the message of salvation by grace through faith in Jesus shows us how righteous he is. Which are we going to focus on? Which seems more relevant? How we see ourselves is paramount.

Following external instructions will not change us—even if those instructions come from Jesus. We have a remarkable ability to treat them like law rather than letting them change us from within. Neither will our knowledge of God's Word change us if it doesn't translate into deep-down faith.

You are not an old creation trying to become new; that's a flawed and frustrating vision and little more than an exercise in acting. You are a new creation shedding the old. Let that sink in, immerse yourself in your vision of Jesus, and see his Spirit working within you. There's no need to try to act like a new creation. You *are* one. Believe it and change will come.

ROMANS 3:21–7:25

THE STORY OF SIN AND FREEDOM

Paul has united Jews and Gentiles in humanity's universal transgression. We are trapped in our fallenness and futility. Now, with a weighty "but now" (3:21), he turns to a much more hopeful topic: a solution that unifies these two groups—and all believers—in faith.

This section of the letter is based on two core truths. First, we gain a right standing with God—or more precisely, God makes our lives right—through our faith. Second, this faith is not confined to one chosen nation but extends to all human beings. It's a universal invitation. The covenant that Jews once thought was exclusive to them is now offered to everyone who believes after the manner of Abraham and in accordance with God's covenant with him. Paul tells Gentiles that they owe a debt of honor to those who first received the promises given to Abraham's descendants. But because these promises are received by faith, not law, everyone has access to them.

To make this point, Paul tells a bit of Abraham's story and how he was declared right and righteous for believing God (chapter 4). But the roots of the redemptive story go back further than that. Paul "retells Adam's tale" (chapter 5).* All human beings inherited sinfulness from Adam; but just as sin entered the world through one person, so does righteousness. By birth, we inherited Adam's sin; by faith (and rebirth), we inherit Jesus' righteousness. Through Jesus, we receive a new nature and entirely new lives (chapter 6). We have died and been buried with Jesus and are resurrected with him. All that once bound us—law, sinfulness, frustration, futility, brokenness, the chains of our fallenness, even our inability to do what's right—no longer has any claim or power over us (chapter 7). We are free.

BACKGROUND

The Gentile world was full of gods, but hardly any made moral claims on their devotees. Because the gods could be demanding and fickle, most pagan worshipers aimed to appease them and curry their favor. Greek and Roman philosophers called people to higher morals, and civic responsibility demanded an effort to do what was right. But the Jewish idea of "rightness" or righteousness—the Greek word implies justice, faithfulness, and true wisdom too—was foreign to many.

How did it work? By most accounts, by following God's laws. But Paul claimed that God's good law couldn't make fallen people good. It simply didn't work on people who had no inherent ability to live up to it. So this strange concept of becoming righteous without following a law or code of ethics was mystifying. If God simply declares you righteous, doesn't that free you to do whatever you want? Conversely, if you can't do whatever you want, doesn't that imply following a law or code of ethics? What's the catch?

Paul replies that this non-libertine, non-legalistic, but still-righteous life is impossible without a radical transformation of human nature. The key is to live according to our transformed nature rather than defaulting to our old one. This takes us out of the legalism/licentiousness conundrum, which cannot lead us to freedom and life. Only a fundamental transformation does.

* Ben Witherington III, *New Testament Rhetoric: An Introductory Guide to the Art of Persuasion in and of the New Testament* (Eugene, OR: Cascade Books, 2009), 131.

THE BIG PICTURE

What's the bottom line for us? Is God merely *calling* us righteous, or can we actually *become* righteous? And because righteousness isn't a universal felt need, what's really at the heart of it? Far beyond becoming better people, we receive a restored relationship with the Creator who designed us for himself and who will fulfill us beyond our greatest hopes.

Righteousness is not defined by what we do or don't do. It's relational, a position of rightness in our relationship with God. As Paul has shown, we can never achieve it. We can only believe God and receive what he has already done for us.

This concept has been widely debated throughout much of Christian history, particularly during the Reformation. Where Martin Luther emphasized an *imputation* of righteousness—a legal, forensic, positional fact applied to us—John Calvin and other reformers embraced an *impartation* of righteousness too. In other words, by our union with Christ, we receive his blessings, the power of his Spirit, and even his divine nature. On that theological foundation, John Wesley, a couple of centuries later, emphasized the experience of holiness or sanctification to an even greater degree. All these views derive from Paul's teaching in Romans, though they differ in their emphases. But Paul's bottom line seems clear: The law can't change our nature. But if our nature is changed, we don't need the law. By faith and dependence on the Spirit within us, we simply live from the new nature we've been given.

To be clear, Paul's teaching is not just about making us righteous, as defined in modern English. It's about making us *right*—which includes being restored into the image of God, reflecting his nature and character, embodying his love, bearing his glory. Our falling short is not so much a matter of failing to live up to a standard as it is a failure to reflect the divine image he endowed us with at Creation. And since Jesus is the perfect representation of that image, the Christian experience necessarily involves being restored into it. That's God's desire for us individually and as a body of believers (8:29-30), and it's where our faith will lead us.

HIS UNSEARCHABLE WAYS

Now God has shown us a way . . . as was promised in the writings of Moses and the prophets long ago.

3:21

This verse represents a turning point in Romans. Some commentators believe the entire letter hinges on 3:21-26, and it's easy to understand why. For one thing, these verses summarize the gospel. For another, they provide a rhetorical bridge over the enormous gap between humanity's problem (from 1:18 to this point) and God's stunning response (the letter from this point forward). Paul has harshly and painfully presented the human condition. Now he turns to the solution. His readers already know the solution, of course—they have believed it. But Paul's explanation is likely more thorough, grounded, and inspiring than they have ever heard.

In this extraordinary salvation, God has shown himself to be "fair and just" (3:26). He has neither swept sin under the rug (which would contradict his perfect righteousness) nor condemned the entire human race for falling short (which would contradict his love and mercy). The law has been satisfied in Jesus, and participation in his death and resurrection—a theme that will soon emerge—gives us life through him. God is both the "just" and the "justifier." In him, both law and grace are fulfilled.

This is why the division between Jew and Gentile no longer exists. And even though that revelation is astonishing—and controversial, as the nation long called to be distinct from all others is now told that those distinctions aren't so important—it was there to be discovered in ancient Scripture all along, promised by Moses and the prophets long ago. God kept his word, even when his people didn't fully understand it.

RE-ENVISION THE POSSIBILITIES

That's good news because we don't fully understand it either. God's Word is complete—but "complete" and "fully comprehended" are not the same thing. We will not find new truth in it, but we will likely find a new understanding of the eternal truth already there. God is faithful to his plan, even when we have tens of thousands of denominations debating its details. Just as the first-century believers marveled at the unfolding of this plan, so will we. And just as his plan stretched their understanding, we should expect it to stretch ours too.

Live with a big vision that recognizes God's ability to transcend our definitions, categories, and debates. Approach Scripture with wonder, seeking the treasures of eternal truth within it. Most of all, rest in God's enormous grace, his immense power, and his limitless creativity to accomplish all he desires.

All have sinned and fall short of the glory of God, and all are justified freely by his grace through the redemption that came by Christ Jesus.

3:23-24, NIV

A year or two before Paul wrote his letter to the Romans, Seneca the Younger, the Stoic philosopher who tutored Nero, wrote that all have sinned and will continue to do so, whether by chance, weakness, or wicked influences.* Philosophers like Seneca made the idea of universal sinfulness familiar to most Romans, who generally would not have disagreed with it. Greek and Roman thinkers knew that we are fundamentally flawed.

Paul's words echo Seneca's, whether intentionally or not, and would not have surprised any of his readers, whether Gentile or Jewish. But he offers something the Greek and Roman philosophers generally did not: a solution. He has so far spent the bulk of his letter arguing that human beings have fallen short of God's glory—colossally, not just a little—but only because he is going to spend the rest of the letter talking about God's glorious response. The depths of our predicament set the stage for the heights of God's purposes. The answer to human futility is an astonishing fulfillment.

Our failure was bigger than sin as most understood it. We didn't just fall short of a standard of righteousness. God endowed us with his image, *and we broke it*! The image was filled with his glory, and we *lost* it. Humanity's

* Seneca, *On Clemency*, written to Nero early in his reign, soon after the young emperor murdered a political rival.

downward descent described in 1:18-32 is not just a behavioral issue; it's a tragic distortion of our original design. The divine image remains in us, but it is distorted. It no longer truly reflects God until we are born of his Spirit and begin growing into his likeness. But that's the power of this gospel. It's the solution for our lost glory, and it positions us to become everything humanity was meant to be.

RE-ENVISION YOUR GLORY

Many Christians don't know we were created for glory. They know we were created to love God and enjoy him forever, but they don't realize that we become *participants* in his glory (John 17:22)—that he made us to display himself to a watching universe.

This is your high and holy calling. To reflect God's glory, you'll need to think glorious thoughts, speak glorious words, and do some glorious things; but that's why he has created you anew and put his Spirit within you. Never be content with the verdict that you have fallen short of God's glory. As part of the human race, that's your past, but your future is brilliant and beautiful. You are becoming a demonstration of the nature of God and nothing short of glorious.

If we emphasize faith, does this mean that we can forget about the law? Of course not! In fact, only when we have faith do we truly fulfill the law.

3:31

Paul mentions faith five times in the last five verses of this chapter, an emphasis meant to contrast the gospel with the law of Moses. We don't achieve righteousness; we receive it. It's a gift from God, whose Son accomplished it on our behalf and then granted it to those who say yes to it by faith.

But as Paul makes clear, being saved by faith is no reason to forget the law. It's how the law is fulfilled within us. God declares us righteous and then empowers us to grow into the truth he has spoken. And because both the legal decree and the practical results come from him, we have nothing to boast about (3:27). From beginning to end, salvation by grace through faith is authored by God. We're simply the beneficiaries.

Does that mean we just wait to get zapped with practical righteousness so we can begin walking in his ways? Of course not. Having come into the Kingdom by faith, we also live by faith. We may struggle for a time to live up to God's nature, but our flesh can never produce the fruit of the Spirit. We may give up trying for a time and trust that grace will cover our shortfalls, but the shortfalls don't reflect God well. Eventually, we understand that even though the law doesn't save us, it isn't irrelevant. The Spirit begins to shape us according to the true purpose of the law.

RE-ENVISION SALVATION

The law is like scaffolding around a gorgeous architectural masterpiece. Once the masterpiece has been built, the scaffolding must be put aside or it will obstruct the view. But its form and intent remain, even when its purpose has been fulfilled.

God did not abandon the law in bringing salvation through Jesus. Jesus himself said he would fulfill the law, not abolish it (Matthew 5:17). God has a greater purpose than human conformity to his standard: human transformation into his likeness.

This is what you and I were designed for—not *acting* like Jesus, which has the effect of another law, but *being* like him. Most Christians are grateful for having been saved from the old life of sin, frustration, and futility; but many still aren't clear on what they were saved *to*. This is it—not just righteousness, but a new state of being that resembles the life of God himself, the breath that first enlivened his original creation and fills us now as we believe. Justification and transformation are vital, but there's an even bigger picture: a restoration of our original design as image-bearers filled with the breath of God. We aren't just being made better; we are being shaped to reflect God as he is.

OUR OPERATING SYSTEM

Abraham believed God, and God counted him as righteous because of his faith.

4:3

Gentiles were likely a majority in the churches in Rome when Paul wrote Romans, but Jews maintained a strong presence there. Both groups would have valued the Hebrew Scriptures (our Old Testament), but for Jews, they were the beginning and end of every discussion about truth. If Paul, a Jewish teacher himself, is going to make any argument about a radical new understanding of salvation, it will have to be thoroughly grounded in Torah. And no case study could be more persuasive than that of Abraham.

Paul has described a decaying, divided humanity in which all creation is degraded, and even though Jews and Gentiles have seemingly lived on separate tracks, they are equally in need of God and his "rightness" or righteousness. Now he turns to a theme of healing humanity and bridging the divides, and he does so by emphasizing the primacy of faith. The rightness and righteousness we need from God have always been received by faith, as the father of Israel makes clear. In other words, even though the very thought is anachronistic, Abraham wasn't a Jew. He was called from among the nations and declared righteous by faith. And this is exactly the God-given means to salvation today, though with a faith specifically anchored in God's saving work through Jesus.

Many rabbis would have agreed with Paul that salvation comes through faith, but they would also have countered that law-keeping and good works are acts of faith. They don't save us, but they are evidence of the faith that does save us. Paul goes further to separate *works* from *faith* (though he would still agree that works are evidence of faith). His point is that Abraham was considered righteous long before the law existed and even before circumcision became a sign of the covenant (Genesis 15:6; 17:9-14). The key condition in making Abraham righteous was his belief in what God promised.

RE-ENVISION GOD'S PROMISES

Faith is the operating system of God's Kingdom, the currency for its transactions, the basis on which his gifts are given and received. Abraham's faith was invested in God's promise of many descendants who would bless the world (Genesis 12:1-3). Our faith is invested in God's promise of eternal life in Jesus. In every case, from these majestic promises to our daily answers to prayer, faith is the key to receiving from God.

Look for God's promises in Scripture—even the ones that apply to a specific situation long ago—and see them as invitations to believe in God's character and purpose. What he has done in the past, he is willing to do again. Scripture is a field manual for life in the Spirit and receiving the Kingdom—not just entrance into the Kingdom, but all Kingdom things. Look beyond natural limitations into supernatural possibilities. Immerse yourself in the very real, but unseen, spiritual world. Pray for God to fill your life with his promises—always in faith that they will be fulfilled.

BELIEVING TRUTH

People are counted as righteous, not because of their work, but because of their faith in God who forgives sinners.

4:5

Everyone has faith. The nonreligious have faith in the idea that there is no spiritual world or that it doesn't matter. The religious have faith that the tenets of their religion are true and important. Committed Christians have faith in Jesus as their Savior. But even with that foundation, faith can turn in all sorts of directions.

Many of us have strong faith in the wrong things. Fear, discouragement, and negativity come from believing false evidence and ideas. Even though Paul will later tell us to consider ourselves dead to sin, many believers have more faith in the power of sin in their lives than in God's power to overcome it. And many Christians receive Christ by faith but live as though their relationship with God is based on performance, feeling unworthy to expect answers to prayer or receive blessings beyond their basic needs. We do live by faith—that's an inevitable part of being human—but our faith isn't always anchored in what God has said.

Paul saw that principle at work in first-century debates about salvation. Many Jews and Christians claimed that their relationship with God was based on faith but then worked as though it all depended on what they did (see Galatians 3:1-14). That's earning wages, not receiving a gift (Romans 4:4). Paul uses an accounting term in verse 5 to describe the righteousness that has been credited to us, then quotes David's words in 4:6-8 to further prove the Old Testament roots of this truth (Psalm 32:1-2). David knew his sins were "covered" not because of works or sacrifices but because he confessed his sin and believed. Our lives do not rest on what we wish for, work for, or think is fair. They rest on what we believe.

RE-ENVISION A CULTURE OF GRACE

We can embrace a divine economy in which works produce righteousness (and exhaust ourselves trying and failing), or one in which we receive grace by faith. Of course, whichever system we choose for ourselves, we must apply to others. We can't receive grace by faith for ourselves while judging others for their works (see Matthew 6:14-15; 18:21-35). It's an all-or-nothing invitation.

Envision the divine economy you want to live in, think about all its implications for yourself and others, and then live in it thoroughly, consistently, persistently, passionately, and unapologetically. Refuse false beliefs about becoming somebody, measuring up, or waiting to "arrive." God has declared that, in Christ, you already are somebody, you have already measured up and have already arrived, and those privileges are open to everyone. See them, live in them, and invite others into them.

Abraham was counted as righteous by God because of his faith. But how did this happen? . . . Clearly, God accepted Abraham before he was circumcised!

4:9-10

You can imagine why Paul's way of thinking was so hard for faithful Jews to accept. For those steeped in God's commandments, living them out as thoroughly as he instructed (Deuteronomy 6:6-9), with the assurance that he had given an everlasting covenant for all generations that would never pass away (Genesis 17:7; Exodus 31:16; Psalm 119:160), the idea of becoming God's people apart from that covenant and its observances was nonsensical. People well-versed in Hebrew Scripture could easily point to passages that affirmed the permanence of the law. And you probably would have assumed that being circumcised and keeping the law represented righteousness.

There are different ways to keep the law, of course—and different motives for doing so. One person might do it to make himself righteous, while another does it simply because he believes what God said. One reflects self-righteousness, the other faith. And by emphasizing the primacy of faith, Paul makes the case that it was primary even before the law—and therefore is now available to Gentiles apart from the law.

Circumcision was a seal of God's approval, not the means to it. Not only did God declare Abraham righteous before he was circumcised; according to Paul, God declared Abraham the father of all who believe apart from circumcision.

That makes him the father of believing Gentiles—a premise that would offend or at least unsettle almost all Jews. But it also explains God's original promise that Abraham's descendants would be a blessing to all nations (Genesis 12:1-3). And it includes countless more descendants—heirs of faith—than many had thought.

RE-ENVISION THE RELATIONSHIP

Even the generation that received the law was told to serve the Lord "with joy and enthusiasm" for benefits already received (Deuteronomy 28:47). That has always been God's desire—not for us to serve him in order to be someone or get something, but because he has already made us someone and given us so much. Circumcision and law-keeping were always meant to be a consequence of righteousness given by God through faith, not the means to get it.

The bigger question is not the Mosaic law—the Gentile church left that debate behind very early—but all the laws the religious instinct still drives us to fulfill. We gravitate toward words to follow rather than a person to know, principles and precepts instead of inner transformation and the investment of time needed for a dynamic relationship with God. Always seek joy and gratitude in the relationship from which all truth, righteousness, and blessings flow.

Clearly, God's promise to give the whole earth to Abraham and his descendants was based not on his obedience to God's law, but on a right relationship with God that comes by faith.

4:13

Paul has written much in the first part of this letter about "a right relationship with God." It is very clear by now that this relationship is based on faith, not on works. We know it doesn't give us license to do whatever we want that may be contrary to God's character, nor does it require us to measure up to a standard. It aims at an inward transformation that works God's character into ours. But even at the beginning of that transformation, when we don't look much different than before, we are declared righteous in God's eyes. He measures us by Jesus' righteousness, not our own.

At this point, it would be fair to ask, "If we are made righteous by grace through our faith in Jesus, how was Abraham considered righteous long before Jesus came into the world? If he could be declared righteous apart from Jesus, why can't we?" It's the same logic Paul has used to prove that Abraham was made righteous apart from the law. Critics could easily exploit that logic to say that Abraham was not only made righteous apart from the law but also apart from Christ.

But the point of Paul's argument isn't to determine a minimum requirement for righteous faith. It's to demonstrate that being counted as righteous for believing God can look different across generations and eras. Because the revelation at Sinai wasn't always the determining factor in the past, it didn't have to be the determining factor going forward. We can conclude that a right relationship with God is based first on believing in him and his plans generally, but also believing in what he has revealed specifically in our time. And in the incarnation, ministry, cross, and resurrection of Jesus—to which all of Scripture has pointed—God's specific revelation about salvation is now clear. Believing this revelation is what makes us right with him.

RE-ENVISION YOUR YES

God is not going to reveal a greater salvation than Jesus, who is the centerpiece, climax, and conclusion of the redemptive plan. But our lives in him are not just about gaining admission to his Kingdom. It's about a whole new kind of existence. The principle of believing God for what he has promised applies to every area of our lives.

Every yes to a word from God—an instruction, a warning, a promise, or anything else—is a righteous statement. Fill your life with those yeses. See every moment as an opportunity to reveal the righteousness of Jesus in you. It's already yours; let every step and every word take you further into that righteousness to experience the fullness of all that God desires for you.

FAITH AND REALITY

Abraham is the father of all who believe . . . "the father of many nations." This happened because Abraham believed in the God who brings the dead back to life and who creates new things out of nothing.

4:16-17

What is faith? This may seem like a basic question, something everyone reading Romans should understand by now. After all, *faith* and *believe* are key words in Jesus' ministry and Paul's explanation of salvation. Yet people in Paul's day and ours struggle to define what faith is. Is it an intellectual agreement with certain facts? A choice to accept something we can't prove to be true? Is it always internal, or does it show outward signs? If our entire relationship with God is based on faith—if we can't please him without it (Hebrews 11:6)—we need to know what it means.

The writer of Hebrews gives us a definition—perhaps not a complete one, but certainly a true one: "Faith is the substance of things hoped for, the evidence of things not seen" (Hebrews 11:1, NKJV). Faith sees beyond the visible realm and into the invisible—an even greater reality than what our natural eyes can discern. It is based on what God has spoken, a concrete expectation that he will bring it to pass. It may be stretched and strained before it is ever fulfilled; it requires us to live as if it has been fulfilled before it has; and it can transcend what is humanly possible. Abraham's case demonstrates all these points. Clearly it's more than just a thought, wish, or assumption. It's the full embrace of a promise from God.

Our faith emphatically declares that God's ability to make us good is greater than our ability to make ourselves good. But it involves believing that he *will* make us good—*even before we see any evidence of change*. He "creates new things out of nothing" (Romans 4:17); or as another translation puts it, he "calls those things which do not exist as though they did" (NKJV). That's important to remember when you consider his declaration of our righteousness—or anything else he says. Faith sees the reality behind appearances.

RE-ENVISION THE EVIDENCE

How can you know if you really believe? Look at your emotions, your plans, and your assumptions. Your feelings won't tell you what truth is, but they will often tell you what you really believe. Your plans are revealing too; if you're praying for provision but planning for lack, you don't really believe provision is coming. And your assumptions eventually show themselves; if you're afraid that your ability to sin is greater than God's ability to keep you from sin or forgive you when you do, you're still focused on yourself.

Notice these signs and keep coming back to faith. Don't be disheartened by what you see. Faith doesn't look for evidence; it *is* the evidence. Stand firm in it, and one day your natural eyes will see what your spiritual eyes have already taken for certainty.

HOPE AGAINST HOPE

Even when there was no reason for hope, Abraham kept hoping—believing that he would become the father of many nations.

4:18

If you've ever waited for the fulfillment of a promise from God, you know how trying the experience can be. For Abraham, it involved years of wondering, second-guessing, filling in the gaps between what God said and what he didn't say, and having his understanding completely reoriented beyond human expectations. Joseph could tell a similar story; from the day he received dreams from God, everything seemed to go tragically in the opposite direction—until one day he discovered that God had been leading him toward the promise all along. Between the time David was anointed as king of Israel and when he actually assumed the throne, he spent years running from a rabid King Saul. And God's people waited centuries for the Messiah to come.

While we're waiting, it's easy to lose sight of hope. In fact, the process is designed to train us in the art of seeing what we don't see and hoping for what is certain but hasn't happened yet. As Paul's words here make clear, there's a strong connection between *hope* and *faith*. As one translation says, "Against all hope, Abraham in hope believed" (4:18, NIV). He became a model of persistent faith that is anchored completely in what God says—against all contrary evidence, including the evidence right before our eyes.

Many Christians today are living without much hope. They have a distant hope for heaven, to be sure, but not necessarily for God to fulfill his promises in the here and now. Unlike David, they have a hard time believing they "will see the LORD's goodness . . . in the land of the living" (Psalm 27:13). They aren't living with much expectancy.

RE-ENVISION HOPE

There's something wrong with that picture. If we really believe all God has said, our lives will glow with hope and joy. Biblical hope is not a mere wish; it's the expectation of something that's certain to happen. God wants us to immerse ourselves in it completely, not just for heaven one day, but for the fullness of life right now—even when life comes with obstacles, problems, and pain. The levels of our hope and joy, even during the long and winding wait for fulfillment, are clear indicators of what we really believe.

Envision the fulfillment of God's promises—all of them, whether here and now or there and then—until they become more real to you than the scenes of your daily life. Let yourself feel the joy of what is coming. Cultivate your heart as fertile ground for faith, and insist on it until it reaches full maturity. Against all hope, in hope believe, and know that God is as pleased with you as he was with Abraham.

FAITH THAT LASTS

Abraham never wavered in believing God's promise. In fact, his faith grew stronger, and in this he brought glory to God. He was fully convinced that God is able to do whatever he promises.

4:20-21

"Abraham never wavered in believing God's promise." It's a startling statement, isn't it? Those who are familiar with Abraham's story in Genesis 12–22 might wish to ask Paul some questions here. Abraham asked how God's promise was possible, proposed alternate solutions, tried to work one out himself (with long-lasting consequences), and laughed (just as his wife did) when God reiterated the promise. All this occurred over many years, during which Abraham and Sarah wrestled with the vision God had given them. Their faith was great, but they didn't come by it easily.

But that isn't what Paul means by *wavering*. God sees the whole story, and Abraham's story ends in faith. That means his faith endured, which also means—from God's perspective—that he didn't falter. That's how God looks at all of our stories—from the vantage point of knowing the end from the beginning. The dips and turns and crises along the way are just part of the journey. Where we end up defines what the journey was all about.

Abraham's story is part of our story as well (Romans 4:23-24). He lived it for our benefit as well as his own. From him, we see what it means to live out a promise—waiting, being stretched, dealing with questions, and waiting some more until the day of fulfillment—and how God is honored in the process. Paul uses Abraham as an example to set up his summary of the gospel in 4:24-25—namely that God will consider us righteous if we believe in him as the one who sent Jesus to die for our sins, and who raised him to life to make us right with him. This is the greatest promise of all, but the dynamics of Abraham's faith apply to every promise God gives his people. Our faith, even if it involves many ups and downs before it matures, brings glory to God.

RE-ENVISION PERSISTENCE

Abraham's promise was about a son and future generations. Ours begins with salvation but may also include guidance, provision, protection, a calling, or anything else God has spoken to his people. Those who measure their faith and God's faithfulness by the ups and downs of circumstances and feelings—whether life seems to be moving toward the promise or away from it—will find their faith growing weaker over time. Those who keep looking to what God has promised will find their faith growing stronger.

We tend to define our relationship with God by how well we think we're doing—which is exactly what many keepers of the law did. But God defines our relationship with him by how thoroughly we've *believed*—as evidenced by our patience and endurance. Miracles happen when faith endures. Persistence is not the sign of a fading promise but of growing faith. And it's essential to the resurrected life God has given us. If our faith is genuine, it grows deep roots in us, transforms us, and persists until it is fully realized. And as it did with Abraham, it glorifies God.

FROM RAGS TO RICHES

Since we have been made right in God's sight by faith, we have peace with God. . . . Christ has brought us into this place of undeserved privilege where we now stand, and we confidently and joyfully look forward to sharing God's glory.

5:1-2

Salvation by grace through faith is about more than justification. Yes, it makes us right with God positionally. And yes, it transforms us as the Spirit works righteousness into us practically. But for people whose hearts are broken and who know they are living in a world of futility, a theology based on spiritual legalities and the call to a changed life doesn't meet a felt need. Thankfully, there is another side to this salvation that does: peace with God, a relational connection that gives us the greatest Friend, Advocate, Supporter, Provider, Protector, and Guide in the universe.

In Scripture, even in the Greek New Testament, *peace* almost always connotes the Hebrew concept of *shalom*, a full and satisfying state that includes wholeness, completion, and fulfillment. In other words, peace with God heals everything Paul has identified in the first three chapters of Romans, all that goes into our brokenness, pain, futility, enmity, and distorted ways of thinking and living. Not only are we no longer at odds with God—that's one of the benefits—but we also experience his fullness and wholeness. That's what the Prince of Shalom (Isaiah 9:6) accomplished in his death and resurrection.

It's worth pointing out that Paul shifts in chapter 5 from a primarily past-tense treatise on the human predicament to a primarily present-tense description of our experience in Christ. Here is where everything changes, and not just incrementally. Brought into a place of "undeserved privilege," we have become a beautiful rags-to-riches story. With our ragged background established earlier in the letter, we now turn to the riches. We may experience some culture shock—we're not used to undeserved privilege, and lingering feelings of unworthiness or a suspicion that it's too good to be true may present serious obstacles. But just as people might adjust over time to a new culture on earth, we adjust to the new life God has given us, and we never stop growing in it. Our new life is glorious.

RE-ENVISION YOUR STORY

To experience your new reality, you will need to spend a lot of time envisioning your life as a rags-to-riches story and begin seeing yourself living in the riches. It's good to know where you came from, but you are no longer there. Get used to living in the mansion, spiritually speaking. You are no longer an orphan off the street; you are one of the Father's favorites, a member of the family, a carrier of his DNA, a true heir of his Kingdom. As Paul says, we share God's glory. False humility that shuns such claims will deprive you of receiving these blessings and the Father of giving them. Like long-lost royalty, step into the universe's royal family and embrace the full inheritance of promises and purposes God has given you in Christ.

BEYOND DISAPPOINTMENT

We can rejoice, too, when we run into problems and trials, for we know that they help us develop endurance . . . character . . . hope. . . . And this hope will not lead to disappointment.

5:3-5

You will experience trials. You already know this because you have certainly gone through some trials and watched other people do the same. Don't make the mistake of thinking God sends trials into your life in order to tempt you; he is not the author of evil (James 1:13). But because we live in the fallen world Paul has so graphically described, trials will come to the saved and unsaved, rich and poor, young and old, and every other category of person you can think of. And though God doesn't author your trials, he will sovereignly use them to grow your faith, along with the hope, character, and endurance that go into it.

Paul has just written about the dynamics of faith, which includes "problems and trials." Because faith implies a gap between belief and fulfillment—or more specifically, between seeing the promise with spiritual eyes and eventually seeing it with our natural eyes—it is almost always stretched, sometimes very uncomfortably. Time plus experience either undermines our faith and hope or increases them. Trials either turn people toward God or away from him. That's just how life works.

But those who allow time plus experience to refine their faith will find that they come away with endurance, character, and the kind of hope that does not disappoint. By faith, all our trials look different because they take us on this journey. They ground us in reality, not the illusion we used to live in. They produce qualities that anchor us in God himself, who will fulfill all his promises and purposes in our lives.

RE-ENVISION TRIALS

The difference between those who grow closer to God through their trials and those who fall away from him is the vision they have along the way—the narrative in their minds as they encounter hardship and cling to hope. Abraham demonstrated this journey of faith through endurance, character, and hope that doesn't disappoint by focusing not on his own or Sarah's body but on the promise God had given (4:19-21). He learned not to consider the visual evidence but to cling to the spiritual reality. God told him to envision the fulfillment (Genesis 15:5; 22:17), and he did.

You cannot depend on natural vision to see supernatural truths and promises from God. Never look for proof of the supernatural in your natural surroundings. Never challenge God's words with your experience; instead, confront your experience with his words. Cling tightly to your God-given vision of hope, let it produce endurance and character, and know he will never ultimately disappoint you.

God showed his great love for us by sending Christ to die for us while we were still sinners.

5:8

Most Greek and Roman philosophers had little use for weakness and humility and advocated helping only those people who deserved help. Worthiness was a high value. But as Paul so often does, he turns common values on their head and shockingly emphasizes God's unfathomable sacrifice for the unworthy.

We don't come across very well in 5:6-11. Paul's words are rather unflattering—we were "utterly helpless . . . sinners" (5:6), condemned (5:9), enemies of God (5:10). But this assessment is actually really good news. If you have ever felt helpless or sinful, as though you were God's problem child, you are a prime candidate for his dramatic intervention. In fact, this is the *only* way to come to God. Jesus didn't come for the righteous; he came for sinners (Mark 2:15-17). He is the remedy for all who fall short, and we gladly fit the description.

When Paul wrote that we were God's enemies (Romans 5:10), he knew from experience. He had zealously tried to put down the Jesus movement by arresting and killing Christians, a background that prompted his self-assessment as the chief of sinners, the "worst of them all" (1 Timothy 1:15). Redeemed from religious hypocrisy and a terrorist mentality and then given an encounter with Jesus and amazing revelations, Paul had experienced the extremes of a believer's rags-to-riches story. He knew the depths of depravity. But he also knew the heights of new life.

RE-ENVISION YOUR RESCUE

We didn't just seek God, decide to believe, and receive the gift of everlasting life in heaven. We were rescued from a dreadful, dire condition in a world of futility and have been transferred into a new kind of life that is fundamentally different from what we've known before, even here in this world. God the Rescuer has broken us free from our natural limitations and brought us into a supernatural reality. In Christ, we are given the opportunity to be radically transformed from fallen, broken creatures to redeemed human beings who share in the divine nature.

That's great news for everyone who thinks they aren't quite "there" yet, who thinks there is still more holiness or righteousness to achieve before entering into God's favor, his blessings, and the super-spiritual feats of highly fruitful missionaries and miracle workers. They hadn't "arrived" yet either; they simply took God at his word. You already have everything you need, and every reason to expect God to bless you fully from the abundance of his grace.

THE DEFEAT OF SIN AND DEATH

The sin of this one man, Adam, caused death to rule over many. But even greater is God's wonderful grace and his gift of righteousness, for all who receive it will live in triumph over sin and death through this one man, Jesus Christ.

5:17

Much of what Paul has written so far has addressed a sense of unfairness in God's plan, specifically that Gentiles who never kept Israel's laws, feasts, and sacrifices were suddenly becoming God's beloved children by faith. All who know the biblical story might also feel that unfairness in Paul's next topic: the entire human race inheriting the sin of our first parents. Death came to all through a tragic fall that happened long before we were ever born. That hardly seems right.

But we can rejoice in the unfairness of another turn of events in human history—that life is available to all through the righteousness and sacrifice of one man. If sin and death can enter the world through one person, so can righteousness and life. We don't do anything to inherit the nature of Adam or Jesus; we are born into both. Adam gave us a gift we'd rather not have. Jesus gave us a gift every human craves. Neither is "fair," but those who have received the latter celebrate it often.

Of course, Jews understood how one could represent all. They experienced this principle every Yom Kippur, when the high priest made a sacrifice on behalf of all the people. They had long understood the idea of one man's sin infecting the entire human race, and God had shown them in their sacrificial system how he would forgive many vicariously through one sacrifice.

Still, many Gentiles then and many people today wonder how the sacrifice of one man two thousand years ago has any relevance to modern life. If we sin individually, how does Jesus' death change how God sees us as individual sinners? That question is relevant in any age, and Paul understands how challenging this idea can be.

RE-ENVISION THE TRIUMPH

If you've thought much about this issue, you may have noticed an interesting phenomenon: For most people, it's easier to believe Adam's sin makes us all sinful than that Jesus' righteousness makes us all righteous. We claim our sinfulness much more often than we claim our righteousness, even though Scripture describes us as no longer sinners but as entirely new creations. This is why Paul will repeatedly emphasize in the next chapter the importance of seeing ourselves as dead to sin and alive to God, no matter what we experience. We have been raised into a new way of seeing specifically so we can live in triumph over sin and death. Cultivate that vision constantly, persistently, even stubbornly until you see the truth of the new you.

THE GREAT REVERSAL

Because one person disobeyed God, many became sinners. But because one other person obeyed God, many will be made righteous.

5:19

In the Old Testament, uncleanness always corrupts cleanness. Touching someone with a physical impurity defiled a person. Handling a dead body made one ritually unclean. "The companion of fools will be destroyed" (Proverbs 13:20, NKJV). A little bad always seemed to mess up the whole lot of good.

Jesus reversed the direction of that influence. He touched people with leprosy and made them clean, healed a bleeding woman without becoming ritually defiled, and hung out with "bad influences" and changed their lives. With him, righteousness and purity trumped sin and impurity. His life undid disease. In the great confrontation between his good and the world's evil, his good won.

We're still told to be careful about negative influences (see 1 Corinthians 15:33; Galatians 5:9), but the point remains, and Paul uses it here. Through Jesus' obedience, many are made righteous. We who were once helplessly sinful, hopelessly stained, and stuck in futility now, by faith in him, become clean, pure, and whole.

This great reversal results in two kinds of humanity: the old and the new, heirs of Adam and heirs of Christ. By default, we are heirs of Adam, but by entering into this union with Jesus by grace through faith, we become his heirs. And this new humanity moves in the opposite direction of old, corrupting, decaying ways. We escape the fallen condition.

RE-ENVISION YOUR HUMANITY

Many Christians are torn between two humanities, believing themselves to be in Christ in principle but seeing themselves as heirs of Adam in practice. We far too easily assume old-humanity limitations because that's what we're used to and that's what we see all around us. But our faith in Jesus opens up all kinds of new-humanity possibilities.

For example, are you a sinner? Not according to Scripture. You're a saint who sometimes sins, but that doesn't make you a sinner any more than good works make a nonbeliever righteous. But if you see yourself as a sinner every time you sin, you will continue to live out that identity. The new-humanity reality is that you don't have to.

It will take time to see yourself in new ways, unfettered by old-humanity expectations and alive to all the spiritual and supernatural possibilities God has given you. Be persistent, saturate yourself in truth, and let God's revelation become more real to you than any other "reality." Jesus has welcomed the new you into all the blessings and benefits of his Kingdom.

Should we keep on sinning so that God can show us more and more of his wonderful grace? Of course not! Since we have died to sin, how can we continue to live in it?

6:1-2

Paul has criticized some of his critics before (3:8), not for misunderstanding the possible abuses of this gospel but for putting words in his mouth that would recommend those abuses. These accusers grasped the meaning of Paul's teaching that salvation by grace through faith firmly establishes us as righteous new creations, regardless of the works we have already done or will do thereafter. As Paul insisted, we who believe are thoroughly, irrevocably clean.

But the critics missed a key point. They assumed that this liberating message was akin to setting criminals free and expecting them to behave out of gratitude for the grace they've been given. But Paul is assuming that the criminal is no longer a criminal—that his nature has been changed, he's been given a new heart, and he will live a lifestyle different from that of his past. The criminal has undergone a metamorphosis and isn't a criminal at all.

To be clear, God's view of sin hasn't changed. The gospel is not some divine "never mind" to all the ways we've fallen short of his glory. He is just as fiercely opposed to sin as he always has been. The difference now is that he has transferred our sin to someone else and expressed his fierce opposition through that person's violent death on a cross. Justice has been served because Jesus stood in our place to receive it.

The whole point is not to just give us a free pass, but to give us a new *life*. These gifts go hand in hand. To take the pass but shun the new life is the kind of abuse Paul rejects. We have died to our former life in the old humanity. Why would anyone try to go back to it?

RE-ENVISION YOUR NEW NATURE

It's sobering that many people do revert to the old way of life. Many Christians send confusing messages—either that sin is a casual matter or that we have the righteousness of Jesus but still need to do much more to become righteous. Our new self gets lost in the confusion.

Be very clear about who you are now. You *are* righteous in your new nature. There is nothing you can do to become more or less righteous. The true you, the resurrected life inside of you, is perfect. But you do have a choice whether to align your thoughts, words, and actions with your new nature. Don't quench the right desires and visions God has placed in you with old-humanity thought patterns and habits. That existence is dead and gone, and to return to it is like walking among the tombs. Open yourself to life in the new creation, even if you experience some culture shock along the way. See yourself as God sees you, and then simply be who you are.

THE EXCHANGED LIFE

Since we have been united with him in his death, we will also be raised to life as he was.

6:5

The great missionary Hudson Taylor once wrote to his sister about his realization of the exchanged life: how fully Jesus took on our identity in his crucifixion and burial and how fully we take on his identity in his resurrection.* How could Christ be rich yet his people poor? How could a banker say to a customer, "You didn't write this check; only your hand did"? If we have been united with Jesus, we are in him, and he is in us. Our old selves died with him, and we rose with him to new life (6:4). Outwardly, we may look just as we did before, but inwardly, Jesus lives his life through us. He took our old nature and its tragic record upon himself and gave us himself in exchange, along with his name, mission, inheritance, authority, and much more. We've entered a radically new reality.

So we are now both dead and alive (6:11), and what remains in us is the life of Jesus and all its fruitfulness: love, truth, joy, purity, power, peace, a supernatural life. So why don't most believers experience the fullness of what is promised here? Largely because we haven't yet fully believed the enormity of it all and aligned ourselves with God's vision. He sees us as righteous, spiritually

* J. Hudson Taylor, letter to his sister Amelia Taylor Broomhall, October 17, 1869. Taylor's understanding and experience of "the exchanged life" is described in Dr. and Mrs. Howard Taylor, *Hudson Taylor's Spiritual Secret* (Chicago: Moody, 1989), 154–164.

empowered, supernaturally alive, members of a new humanity that far transcends the old. We generally don't. We look at the remnants of our old lives as if they define us. We focus on our flaws, regret our mistakes, and lament our inability to change no matter how hard we try. But as we know from experience, trying harder isn't the answer. Experiencing real change comes from seeing and believing differently.

RE-ENVISION YOUR SOURCE

Ask God to let you see yourself as he does, and don't argue with him when he begins to answer. ("Yes, but didn't you see what I did last week? Don't you know how weak I am?") You will soon see the life of Jesus working through a beautiful new creation, just as a flourishing vine enlivens its fruitful branches (John 15:5). You will see your prayers not as your own but as his—offered in his name, with his status and credit score attached. You will accept the uncomfortable fact that you are a saint, a holy one, treasured and loved, just as Paul assures his readers at the beginning of most of his letters (as in Romans 1:7). If your heart can embrace what your mind objects to, you will know you are the delight of his eyes. And all the blessings that flow through Jesus will flow through you too.

OUR PERSONAL RENAISSANCE

When we died with Christ we were set free from the power of sin.

6:7

The prophet's words were very clear. The human heart is desperately wicked and deceitful, and leopards don't change their spots (Jeremiah 17:9; 13:23). But prophets also prophesied profound, genuine change and said we would be given a new heart (Jeremiah 24:7; Ezekiel 11:19; 36:26-27). Apparently, these leopards do change. We aren't stuck in "desperately wicked" forever. And it only makes sense; why would any salvation given by God leave us in that condition?

God's solution to our desperate problem was not to improve our condition. It was to take our old nature into the grave with Jesus and leave it there. What comes out of the grave is a shared life with Jesus that is incorruptible, powerful, and free. The gospel message is not about an improved self or even a radical reformation. It's a renovation, a renaissance, a renewal of the highest order. We have died and been made alive as something new, never to die again.

If you're like most Christians, you probably don't see yourself as free from sin. You may believe you are free from the penalty of sin, but the idea of being free from the power or practice of sin is a much harder sell. That's what happens when we look at the evidence through natural eyes. But which is a more certain statement of reality: the visual evidence you see or what God says about you?

Until the latter takes root in your heart—granted, it's a process—you will probably feel defeated by your own shortfalls. You'll believe in the freedom of the new humanity while experiencing the futility of the old. Meanwhile, God invites you and all of us to live in the resurrection today.

RE-ENVISION TRANSFORMATION

It's impossible for a cat to turn into a dog, but imagine if one wanted to try. Even if it miraculously learned how to bark, pant, dig, and whimper, it would still not be a dog. It wouldn't have the impulses, instincts, personality, or nature of a dog. It would just be a cat acting like a dog. Playing the part doesn't change anything.

We can try to act like Jesus in our old nature—the one that's supposed to have died—but that just makes us people who act like Jesus, not people who *are* like him. Our transformation into his likeness can only happen supernaturally. Acting a part is exhausting. Being infused with new life is energizing. In complete faith and trust, ask God daily to bring about an infusion of his life within you. Then constantly envision yourself living by it.

CONSIDER IT SO

You also should consider yourselves to be dead to the power of sin and alive to God through Christ Jesus.

6:11

Beware the narratives in your own mind. If you're like most people, many of those narratives aren't very complimentary. Some anticipate problems that never come about. Some rehearse past mistakes and embarrassments that ought to remain in the past. Some convince us of an identity God never gave us or a trait we've been conditioned to accept: *I always mess things up. I'm terrible at self-discipline. I'm too shy and socially inept to influence people. I always say the wrong things. I'm . . .* You can fill in the blank with whatever applies to you. Your personal narratives almost certainly already have.

None of these thought patterns are appropriate in the new humanity, yet we unwittingly train ourselves in them constantly. We're reluctant to believe the best because "it might not be true," but we easily believe the worst even when it's untrue. Changing these thought patterns requires a process of renewal—which Paul will address later—but here he presents the solution: "Consider yourselves . . ." This applies to so many areas of our lives, especially living from our new nature.

The difference between seeing ourselves through the lens of the old nature (which must be turned toward Christ, watched suspiciously because the heart is desperately wicked, disciplined to obey, and inspired to live differently) and the lens of the new nature (in which the old is dead and gone and we are new creations, born of an incorruptible spirit through resurrection with Christ) shapes everything. One is a Christian life that feels like walking through mud; some progress is made, but it's also filled with confusion, deception, corruption, and ongoing sin. The other is like putting on new clothes and just living in that new persona. Like a cross-cultural missionary who identifies with the people of his host culture, we take on new ways of living, and over time, it becomes natural.

We've been given the righteousness of Christ but often experience sin anyway, creating a gap between the biblical reality and its fulfillment in our lives. Still, we have a choice. Are we going to consider ourselves alive to sin or dead to it? The evidence is irrelevant. Everything God says is true. Believing that truth—stubbornly, persistently, deeply—we grow into the reality of our righteousness over time.

RE-ENVISION YOUR NARRATIVES

Paul presents a principle that applies not only to the immediate context of his words but also to everything God says about us: *Consider it so*. We are to see ourselves as God says we are—here, as dead to sin. Paul knows that if this vision is deeply rooted within us—if in every situation we instinctively know, without second-guessing, that our former relationship with sin is broken, dead, and gone—we will live accordingly. If we don't know that—if past experience and present uncertainty whisper to us that we are still very much alive to sin—we will continue to walk in it because we always live from our perceived identity. If we see ourselves as sinners (even sinners saved by grace), we will live out the identity of a sinner. If we see ourselves as righteous, we will grow into that identity. It's a powerful principle for any truth God gives us: Whichever of his gifts and promises we consider to be true *in fact* eventually become true in our experience.

CONSIDER AND PRESENT

Do not let any part of your body become an instrument of evil to serve sin. Instead, give yourselves completely to God, for you were dead, but now you have new life. So use your whole body as an instrument to do what is right for the glory of God.

6:13

The idea of a "life debt"—serving someone who saved your life because, without that lifesaving act, your life would have been over—is a rich theme in fiction, but it's also a good picture of what we owe Jesus. Paul points to it here and elsewhere (1 Corinthians 6:19-20). By taking our old lives into the tomb with him and bringing us out with a new life, Christ has saved us and we owe him everything.

In our indebtedness to Jesus, and in light of the fact that we consider our old nature dead and gone (regardless of what we see with our natural eyes), Paul urges us to give ourselves *completely* to God—literally, to *present, offer, place before* him every part of us. Pairing this instruction with that of Romans 6:11, we now hold a powerful catalyst to a changed life: *consider* and *present*. Paul will later tell us to let our minds be renewed (12:2), and these are two vital components of that renewal. Both are acts of faith and require vision, and with them Paul reaffirms that we don't just enter into this new life by believing but continue to live it out by believing too. Salvation is not just a ticket to heaven. It's comprehensive of our entire lives.

Presenting ourselves—or more specifically, our "members" (ESV, NKJV)—to God is only logical. Otherwise, we're saying we believe we have new life but are choosing to live out the old one. When we present ourselves to God, we are making a statement of faith that he can transform us. We release ourselves from the burden of becoming better and cast it onto him as the one who can make it happen. And to the degree that we continue to offer ourselves to him, he will.

This is where the critiques we saw at the beginning of the chapter break down. The critic thinks we'll keep sinning if we don't have rules in place. Paul thinks we'll align ourselves with the righteousness we've been given because we've been changed. If we stop with the rule-keeping and learn to "consider and present," we will, over time—and sometimes even rapidly—become more closely aligned with God.

RE-ENVISION OBEDIENCE

There are two different interpretations of doing God's will—obedience to outer instructions and standards, or living out our new nature organically. Obedience to instructions and standards is a kind of legalism, and it's far better than sin. But it isn't ideal. God's goal is to transform us so thoroughly that we don't even have to think about standards. We just live out of our new nature. Paul calls this "wholeheartedly" obeying, or being "obedient from the heart" (6:17, NLT, ESV, NASB). If we're obeying God against our inner inclinations in some area of life, we should see that obedience as a sign that we need more transformation in that area. Over time, we should see those signs with less frequency.

Envision your life of presenting yourself to God as a form of discipleship on a spectrum, with obedience to outward instructions (even Jesus' words) at one end and inward transformation at the other. Obedience against your natural inclinations will be necessary at times, but remember the ultimate goal: to be transformed and then just live. Move toward the liberating end of the spectrum with an ever-renewing heart.

THE OBEDIENCE SPECTRUM

ROMANS 7:14-25

OLD NATURE

OBEDIENCE *AGAINST* NATURE

Fallen humanity can only obey laws, rules, precepts, and principles through self-discipline and willpower, training the old nature to behave in new ways but without inner transformation. This obedience is far better than disobedience but always results in obeying God against our inner inclinations.

ROMANS 8:5-14; 12:2

NEW NATURE

OLD NATURE

OBEDIENCE *FROM* NATURE ⟶ OBEDIENCE *AGAINST* NATURE

When we believe in Jesus, we are resurrected to new life with him and given a new nature that is without sin. Whether we cultivate and rely on that new nature is up to us—many Christians have a new nature but still try to reform the old one—but we *can* do it, as Paul describes in Romans 8:5-14 and 12:2. When we find ourselves obeying God against our nature, we can take it as a sign that we need more transformation in that area. This lifelong process of discipleship will include self-discipline but is dependent on the Holy Spirit for the power to change. Where we once tried to obey entirely from the old nature (because that's all we knew), our obedience from our new nature now *increases*, and obedience against our old nature diminishes. To the degree we are transformed, we can live from our natural inclinations, which now align with the Spirit.

ROMANS 6:12-14

NEW NATURE

OLD NATURE

OBEDIENCE *FROM* NATURE

The picture Paul gives us in Romans 6 is of a life completely transformed—dead to sin and made alive through the resurrection of Jesus. This is objectively true of us now, but we experience our transformation over time. Complete, experiential transformation, in which we live entirely from our new nature—not out of conscious obedience but simply because we have been changed—is our ultimate goal, though we can only approach it increasingly in our earthly lifetime. In our glorified state, we will be fully restored into the image of God, who needs no law or standard because his nature is perfect.

A CHOSEN CAPTIVITY

Sin is no longer your master, for you no longer live under the requirements of the law. Instead, you live under the freedom of God's grace.

6:14

We were created to devote ourselves to someone or something. Even fiercely independent people find themselves serving their careers, interests, or romantic partners. We talk about some people being slaves to their work, the opinions of others, old ways, details, or even fashion. Many of these "enslavements" are purely voluntary, and we enter into them because we were made to serve.

The good news is that we get to choose our captivity. Paul says we are slaves to whatever we choose to obey (6:16); but by virtue of our faith in Jesus for the salvation that comes through his death and resurrection, we no longer have to be enslaved to the corruption and futility of this world or our own fallenness. We can choose a far more liberating "captivity" by offering ourselves to Jesus.

Non-Christians (and even many Christians) assume that this new captivity to Christ will be exhausting, constricting, and soul-crushing because it means obeying standards we don't like and can never live up to. Humanity's religious instinct always positions faith and devotion this way because it's focused on what we do to reach God, not what he has done to reach us. But a relational transformation is drastically different. God is writing his truth, his will, and even the spirit of his law into our hearts (Jeremiah 31:31-34; Ezekiel 11:19-20; Hebrews 10:14-18). We're not depleted by trying to live out his calling. Instead, we enter into our new nature, our true selves. We get to be who we are.

RE-ENVISION CHRISTLIKENESS

Remember the futility of a cat trying to become a dog. That's how many people approach Christianity. But acting like Jesus doesn't make you Christlike. *Being* like Jesus does. For example, you can love others because you're told to or love them because you're a loving person. You can act with integrity because it's the right thing to do or act with integrity because you have it. These are not minor distinctions. There's an enormous difference between doing the right thing because it's right and doing the right thing because you're righteous.

When raw obedience is all you can muster, do that. It's far better than disobedience. But the journey of faith is a matter of moving from obedience *against* your nature to obedience *because* it's your nature—from behavioral change to heart transformation. One is as tiring as keeping the law. The other is wholly liberating and will demonstrate to the world the power of the gospel.

FREE TO BE

Now you are free from the power of sin and have become slaves of God. Now you do those things that lead to holiness and result in eternal life. For the wages of sin is death, but the free gift of God is eternal life through Christ Jesus our Lord.

6:22-23

Paul is writing to Gentile and Jewish believers who are still learning what it means to be Christians, but he takes for granted that they have already been set free. That's because the journey of faith is not about becoming something we are not. It's about uncovering what we were designed to be and have already become. Our spirit has already been reborn. We have already been given a new nature. We have already received a righteousness that bears the fruit of eternal life. The reborn spirit that God has put within us is perfect. Living it out in practice is a matter of relying on the Holy Spirit and the gift of righteousness and getting rid of whatever doesn't align with them. But our reborn spirit is there, it's immutable, and we can live in it today.

Yes, we still exhibit some imperfections, but those are vestiges of what we once were. Thought patterns are deeply ingrained in us, habits persist, and relational dynamics present us with frequent triggers to return to old ways of communicating. But why dwell on them? Why be preoccupied with our flaws when we can be rapturously fascinated with the perfection of our new nature?

We'll never overcome old ways by focusing on them. That will only ingrain them in us further. Freedom comes through filling our vision with the new ways that replace the old.

RE-ENVISION GOD'S NATURE

Consider God's nature. Does he obey his own law? Is he bound by its terms? Is he free to do whatever he wants? These questions do not suitably frame God's nature. They are hardly relevant because God simply is who he is. He neither obeys the law nor disobeys it because he doesn't need it as a reference point. He *is* the reference point. He needs no restraints on his thoughts or behavior. He freely lives out his own nature.

By being united with Jesus, we have entered into the same kind of freedom. As a man, Jesus theoretically could have sinned. He could have rebelled against his own nature. When we sin as believers, that's exactly what we're doing. Jesus made obedient choices in the flesh, but that obedience flowed from who he is. Even so, we too have been made alive by union with the resurrected Jesus, who now lives in heaven beyond the world's temptations. As deity, a member of the Trinity, he freely lives out his own nature. And by being united with him, so can we.

But to do so, we have to know our new nature, consider the old one dead, present every part of ourselves to God, rest in what Jesus has accomplished for us, rely on his Spirit, and be who we were made to be. Let that prospect capture your imagination. Dream about what it looks like. Envision the implications. And go into your world in the complete freedom of an altogether new kind of being.

BETTER THAN A CODE

So, my dear brothers and sisters, this is the point: You died to the power of the law when you died with Christ. And now you are united with the one who was raised from the dead. As a result, we can produce a harvest of good deeds for God.

7:4

When a man named Wyatt, who had a wife and six children, was drafted to fight in the Civil War, a younger man named Pratt offered to go in his stead, using Wyatt's name. Pratt died in battle, and when the authorities realized he wasn't Wyatt, they tried to draft Wyatt again. But Wyatt insisted that he had already died in battle—as the records showed—even though his death was suffered by another man. According to the law, "*he had died in the person of his representative.*"*

This illustration captures the essence of our vicarious death and resurrection through Jesus. We didn't experience the Cross and the Resurrection, but we participate in them. We are joined to Jesus in both. He is our representative who carried out the transaction, the exchanged life, himself. It's a powerful picture of our rebirth.

Paul understood the power of vision in changing our lives. In describing our new life in Christ, he has given us several word pictures: being buried and resurrected with Christ (6:3-11); our oppressive enslavement to sin versus our

* L. E. Maxwell, *Born Crucified* (Chicago: Moody Press, 1945), 13. Italics in the original.

liberating enslavement to God (6:15-23); and here (in 7:1-3), a surviving spouse who lives past the bonds of marriage. Just as a wife is no longer bound to a husband who has died, we who believe are no longer bound to the law—not because the law has died but because we have. That death ends the relationship. Obligations have been fulfilled. Jesus took our old, failed commitment to the grave and came out with a new covenant of life.

"Now we are released from the law, having died to that which held us captive, so that we serve in the new way of the Spirit and not in the old way of the written code" (7:6, ESV). Neither Israel's law nor any other can hold us to its standard. We have something much better than a code to live by.

RE-ENVISION UNION WITH JESUS

The image of being baptized into Jesus' death and resurrection is life changing—and it's more than simply a metaphor. A real transaction took place in that exchange. Christ became everything we are so we could become everything he is, as the exact image of God in a man. We don't become members of the Trinity or create our own worlds, but we do become one with God and share his creative power and nature (John 17:21-22; 2 Peter 1:4). We are inextricably bound to, merged with, and dependent upon Jesus and his life within us.

Just as God designed marriage for fruitfulness, so our relationship with Jesus produces fruit. Begin each day with a vision of Jesus living through you. His mission, ministry, presence, power, gifts, works, faithfulness, favor, fruitfulness, and even his name are yours. Embrace your new identity fully. Let Jesus be Jesus in you.

SIN VERSUS THE LAW

Sin used this command to arouse all kinds of covetous desires within me! If there were no law, sin would not have that power.

7:8

Is the law bad? This is the primary question Paul addresses in chapter 7, and it's an understandable one in light of his many statements about the law's inability to produce righteousness—and its ability to provoke sin, as he will soon elaborate upon.

How can a good tree produce bad fruit? Here Paul insists that it hasn't. Because God gave the law, it is good and true (7:12). But when this good and true law was revealed, humanity in its broken, fallen condition rebelled against it, and in that gap between the good law and a rebellious people, sin was revealed and even produced.

Since his great declaration that he is not ashamed of the gospel (1:16), Paul has only referred to himself in passing a couple of times. In 7:7, the emphasis on "we" and "you" in previous chapters now turns to "I" and "me," and we aren't sure why. His statement in 7:7 that he wouldn't have known coveting was wrong without the law seems to contradict his previous claim that even Gentiles have an innate sense of right and wrong (1:21, 32). How did the law against coveting produce coveting (7:8) when Gentiles who didn't have the law still coveted (1:29)? We might have reason to think Paul isn't necessarily talking about himself in this passage.

Putting oneself in the place of another was a common rhetorical device, and Paul may have been taking on the voice of all who are outside of Christ, humanity born of Adam, the biblical figure he has most recently mentioned (5:12-21) and the only man who was alive before sin killed him (7:9-11). He can't be taking on the voice of Jews; he has gone to great lengths to place Jews and Gentiles in the same position. In one way or another, whether in his own experience or all of humanity's, the law shone a bright light on our fallenness while also illuminating God's perfection.

RE-ENVISION SIN

The good news in this passage, which Paul will develop throughout the rest of the chapter, is that sin is a separate entity working against us, not part of our nature as believers. Paul's insistence that we are new creations endowed with the righteousness of Christ raises the objection in most readers that we still experience sin working within us. But Paul writes of sin as an invasive force. It's not *us*. It's *against* us.

Far too many believers feel guilty about being tempted (even though Jesus himself was tempted), as if temptation springs from our own nature. Yet Romans and the rest of the New Testament are clear. Before salvation, we had a sinful nature. After salvation, we do not. Old things have passed away (2 Corinthians 5:17). We have the righteousness of Christ. There is no dual occupancy of our souls. We have one nature, and insofar as sinners do good works or the righteous sin, we entertain forces that are foreign to us. Refuse to give sin a place of honor as part of your identity or nature. Learn to see it as an intrusive, alien element, and you will be far more empowered to reject it and overcome its attacks.

BEYOND SIN MANAGEMENT

What a miserable person I am! Who will free me from this life that is dominated by sin and death? Thank God! The answer is in Jesus Christ our Lord.

7:24-25

Even Roman and Greek writers expressed frustration over the human condition, and in the second half of chapter 7, Paul does too. He has already declared that all believers have been set free (6:22), and he will declare it again at the beginning of the next chapter (8:1-2). But in between, he laments that he doesn't do the good he wants to do and does do the wrong he doesn't want to do (7:17-23). He feels so stuck in this conundrum that he calls himself a "miserable person," a "wretched man" (NIV, ESV, NKJV, NASB). He is in an agonizing state.

This wretchedness does not fit any of Paul's descriptions of the Christian life anywhere else—in fact, he emphatically and repeatedly declares the joy and freedom of that life, even in this letter—so it defies all he has written to suggest that this kind of captivity to sin is his Christian experience. Is he talking about his past experience, along with that of everyone else who has tried to become righteous without the power of the Spirit and a Kingdom worldview to transform them? Is he still speaking in the voice of all humanity under Adam? Is this the voice of a pious Jew falling short of the law? As much as we may relate to this struggle—and most people do at some point in their lives—it is not a picture of the new humanity's freedom in the Spirit. It's an old-humanity conundrum, even if we experience it in the new creation.

This age-old human dilemma is universal, even for Jews under the covenants of Abraham and Moses. We all have ideals we can't live up to, and we especially fall short of God-given ideals. Fallen humanity has no ability to live the unfallen life, yet that's the kind of life we were created to live. We were stuck in our condition with apparently no way out.

But in the new creation, sin does not dwell within us as it did in our old condition (7:20, 23). It may pose as an internal force and in that sense work within us, but it is deceptively coming from outside our new selves. It may be working in us, but it isn't *us*. Whenever we think it is—when we let our experience define our identity—we get trapped in this same frustration.

Paul is describing a life of sin management—trying to deal with sin in the strength of fallen flesh, a non-believing approach (even when believers do it). The gospel is not about managing sin; it's about leaving it behind. We can never overcome the flesh in the strength of the flesh. We need the power of the Spirit and the true image he gives us in order to do so. New behaviors that are not solidly built on a new foundation of identity, relationship, purpose, and destiny simply are not going to last. That's why so many Christians are still stuck in the Romans 7 conundrum, which is based on a legalistic approach to Scripture, even the Scripture that is the New Testament.

RE-ENVISION YOUR PREDICAMENT

As believers in God's revealed Word, we know he gives us a new identity (a new way of seeing ourselves), an entirely new relational context (as God's sons and daughters and each other's brothers and sisters), a new purpose (a new way of seeing our reason for being), and a new destiny (a new vision of eternity). Still, when many of us read the Bible, we look at it through the lens of what we "should" be doing. We want to cut to the chase of practical application before we've learned to rely on the Spirit. And that instinct traps us in misery.

Give immensely more attention to *being* than *doing*. Doing without being is pure futility. Through being, the doing will come. Catch a vision of your new, transformed nature, celebrate it, give thanks for it, and dance in the freedom it gives. Your life will reflect the new creation you have become.

ROMANS 8

NEW LIFE, FUTURE GLORY, ENDURING LOVE

Paul has been rather methodical in his argument up to this point, but chapter 8 is a virtual explosion of insights into the implications of what he has written. He has made the case that everyone—Jew and Gentile—is rightfully under judgment in our natural fallen condition, and no amount of human willpower, effort, good deeds, creativity, or ingenuity gives us a way out of this futile existence. But there *is* a way out, and Paul has already presented it: the Good News of salvation by grace through faith, in which God justifies people who believe (even Gentiles with no experience in Jewish laws, feasts, rituals, and worship), while remaining just himself. He has not broken, ignored, or eradicated his covenant; he has fulfilled it in Jesus. Instead of keeping the covenant ourselves, we enter into Jesus' covenant keeping. His life is now ours.

If we had to identify the major theme in this chapter—and there are several big ones—we might call it the chapter of the Holy Spirit. Paul gets specific about the Spirit's role in our new life. He has used the word *spirit* (in reference to ours or to God's) only five times up to this point in the letter, but he uses it twenty-two times in chapter 8 alone. This chapter is an unveiling of what life in the Spirit entails.

It begins with a resounding declaration that there is no condemnation for those who are in Christ (8:1) and proceeds to describe his life within us. We can choose to fill our minds with either futile, fleshly, mundane thoughts or with matters of the Spirit. The thoughts and works of fallen humanity all go to the grave, while the thoughts and works of the Spirit empower us with life and bear eternal fruit (8:5-13). If we have God's Spirit within us, we are his children, heirs with Jesus of all he inherits (8:12-17). But his inheritance comes with some suffering for now, especially as the creation we live in groans for redemption, longs for a revelation of who we are, and looks ahead with us toward our resurrection (8:18-25). When we pray for this world and anything else, the Spirit and the Son pray with us in agreement with the Father's will (8:26-27, 34). And the Father works on our behalf and with us to bring about good in all things, including our transformation into bearers of his glorious image (8:18, 28-29). We have therefore overcome all the fallenness, futility, and frustration of this world, and even the world itself, and therefore no power or problem exists that can separate us from the love of God, which surrounds us in Jesus (8:31-39).

BACKGROUND

This beautiful picture of redemption, renewal, and restoration—all three are integral to the promise of salvation—is painted against the backdrop of empty promises from an earthly kingdom. The emperor cult was thriving in Paul's day as the Caesars were increasingly being identified as "sons of god," or at least semi-divine, and honored as "lords." The "good news" of Caesarean rule, the Pax Romana (Roman peace), seemed to represent a new era in human history in which justice, order, peace, security, glory, and even salvation (a word Romans applied to their imperial rule) flourished. But these benefits came at a heavy price—not the suffering of those who ushered in this era of history, but the suffering of those who resisted it. This peace was achieved and maintained by violence—including the violence done to a certain Jewish Messiah.

Paul is talking about a different peace brought about by a different Lord through suffering (actually inflicted by Rome but representative of a world hostile to God). Elsewhere, he writes of Jesus disarming the powers through his crucifixion. Romans 8 (and much of Scripture) is a counter-narrative to the world's promises and claims. It's a picture of the new humanity.

THE BIG PICTURE

At its heart, this portrayal of new life in chapter 8 is a restoration of what we lost in Eden—God working with and through his people to express his loving care over the world. And the only way we can reflect God in this world is by being restored to the original image we were given, which is fully expressed in Christ, into whose likeness we are now being conformed (8:29-30). This restoration is so much fuller than simply being made morally righteous, as important as that is. We certainly do become moral, but even more significantly, we become like our Father, just as the Son perfectly represents him.

What does it mean to be God's adopted heirs? It involves the freedom and power of life in the Spirit, but also suffering, becoming a revelation of God's nature for the world to see, praying with him (not just *to* him), and living in overwhelming victory, overcoming the dangers and destructiveness of this world. In other words, it resolves the crisis of the human condition, which is even more broadly a crisis of God's creation. In the words of N. T. Wright, our "salvation is not just God's gift *to* his people, it is God's gift *through* his people"* to a world groaning to escape its own futility.

Your salvation, therefore, is not only what *you* need as a fallen human being; it's also what the world needs from you. Creation longs for your transformation—the glory and love revealed in those who believe, and the promise that human fallenness is not the end of our story. As a bearer of the image of the King of kings, you become a living, breathing outpost of the Kingdom, a carrier of its promises and blessings. You have become part of the universe's symphony of praise, honor, and glory to your Creator. You may feel as if you're playing a solo at times, but from the vantage point of heaven, it's one part of a beautiful whole.

* N. T. Wright, *Into the Heart of Romans: A Deep Dive into Paul's Greatest Letter* (Grand Rapids: Zondervan Academic, 2023), 6.

NO CONDEMNATION

Now there is no condemnation for those who belong to Christ Jesus.

8:1

Heavy condemnation for all of humanity, whether Jew or Gentile, fills the first few chapters of Romans. This grim assessment climaxes at the end of chapter 7 with a picture of miserable futility and frustration. Even those who want to do good find themselves incapable of it; all are bound to sin and its wages of death.

But at the beginning of chapter 8, Paul breaks through this condemnation with a breathtaking claim that there is no condemnation for those who are in Christ. It's all wiped away. All those heavy accusations against us, all that depravity and darkness, all the failures to live according to law, conscience, or any other right and good standard, are removed, never to be held against us again. Having recited our collective offenses and the charges against us in God's universal court of justice, Paul declares innocence for all who believe.

He has presented this truth already—this essential argument has been threaded in and out of the discussion since 3:21—but notice the comprehensive nature of the claim as he states it here. Paul could have said there is no condemnation for those who continue to walk in the Spirit (as many have interpreted his words in 8:6 and 8:13), or that there is no condemnation for believers who have progressed to a certain level, achieved a certain degree of maturity, or remained consistent in their faith. Instead, he insists there is *no* condemnation for *anyone* who is in Christ. True to his teaching earlier in the letter, freedom from condemnation has nothing to do with works and everything to do with being in Christ by faith. We really are given a clean slate, and because it depends entirely on God's work in Christ, the slate is never made unclean again.

RE-ENVISION YOUR INNOCENCE

You might not think of yourself as innocent—you know your past better than anyone—but God's verdict is that you are *not guilty* by virtue of Jesus' life, death, and resurrection. He fulfilled the law—he accomplished what the miserable man of Romans 7 could not—and then he gave his spotless record to those who have been united to him by faith. There is no stain on you.

Imagine the exhilarating sense of freedom someone sentenced to life in prison would feel if they were suddenly declared innocent of all crimes, with all future charges dropped. That's the gift God has given us, and not in place of a life sentence but of an eternal one. God will never impose on us an impossible standard again. We are empowered—and forever free—to do whatever he calls us to do and experience the fullness of joy in doing it.

FREEDOM FOR LIFE

Because you belong to him, the power of the life-giving Spirit has freed you from the power of sin that leads to death.

8:2

The condemned have been set free from the penalty of their crimes. But what if they still have criminal inclinations? It's one thing to be delivered from consequences, quite another to be delivered from the dysfunction and behaviors that created the trouble in the first place. If people are by nature drawn to crime, freedom will only facilitate more of the same. Freedom is hardly a gift if lives still spiral downward.

But our freedom in Christ does more than wipe away our record and get us out from under the debts we owe. It empowers us to live as people who never deserved those debts to begin with. God has set us free through the work of Jesus, but he enables us to live free through the work of the Spirit. We have entered into a separate sphere, a new reality, a life that draws from an eternal source. It is already ours.

It's worth noting that Paul uses the present tense in the previous verse (8:1)—there *is* no condemnation—and switches to past tense in 8:2-4. We live now in what God has *already* accomplished. We don't strive to enter in; we simply receive it. Because God has done a great work, we enter into a great rest.

The Spirit has first produced the kind of faith that gives life—the focus of Paul's message so far—but his presence in us also produces the kind of faith that shapes and sustains life. The old Reformers' bedrock truth that "the just shall live by faith" (1:17, NKJV) can be taken to mean that we *receive* life by faith and/or we *live* life by faith. The Spirit works both truths deeply into our lives as we follow him rather than our old sinful nature (8:4-5). We are not left to our own willpower and self-discipline to live out our freedom. That would hardly be freeing at all. We lift our sails to catch the wind of the Spirit and move in his ways.

RE-ENVISION EMPOWERMENT

Imagine exhausting yourself for years trying to overcome sin and failing repeatedly, piling on guilt and shame for your constant shortcomings. It's a common experience, and multitudes of Christians can relate to it. No matter how hard you try—or how often you succeed—the eventual slipups keep you deflated. You never quite arrive.

Now imagine those slipups and shortcomings as soiled napkins. You don't focus on the dirt attached to them, try to figure out what went wrong, or bring them back out to rehash again and again. No, you throw them away and move on. That's how we deal with something that is no longer relevant to our lives. We leave it behind without a second thought.

It feels irresponsible to leave sin behind like that, but if God has separated us from our sins as far as the east is from the west (Psalm 103:12), it's actually irresponsible to keep them near in our thoughts. Let them go. Envision your freedom, wholeness, and God-given righteousness in their place, and move in every direction the Spirit takes you.

A MATTER OF MINDSET

Those who live according to the flesh set their minds on the things of the flesh, but those who live according to the Spirit set their minds on the things of the Spirit. For to set the mind on the flesh is death, but to set the mind on the Spirit is life and peace.

8:5-6, ESV

God has given us a new nature, and it isn't inherently sinful. But as every Christian has experienced, we can still sin. That intrusive, hostile entity that works against us through old thought patterns, habits, relational dynamics, misconceptions, and self-focus has no power other than the power we give it, but we often empower it anyway. In spite of God's extravagant gift of freedom, most of us don't know how to live in freedom.

These verses (and 8:13) can be frightening if misread as a warning that our eternal destiny depends on whether we set our minds on the Spirit consistently. This tenuous hope of eternity goes against everything Paul has taught, and it raises the question of how much is enough. No believer sets their mind on the Spirit perfectly, and our salvation can't depend on a constantly changing success rate. There's no freedom in that.

Paul's point is that the mind set on the flesh will always lead to things that end: temporary, decaying, unfulfilling pursuits. But the mind set on the Spirit will always lead to things that last: eternal, fruitful, life-giving pursuits. For those who aren't born of the Spirit and never let him drive their thoughts, everything in their life leads to death. But those born of the Spirit, who have at least sometimes let him drive their thoughts, even if inconsistently, are being rooted in eternity and experiencing something of its blessings even now.

Many Christians still feel stuck in guilt and shame because they are setting their minds on the flesh—even to defeat it—rather than on the Spirit. Religious effort—raw willpower, self-discipline not aided by the Spirit—can create an obsession with sin, which will always have the opposite effect from what we want. Focusing on the flesh in an effort to overcome its power is still focusing on the flesh, and Paul has made it very clear that the flesh cannot overcome the flesh. The only way to overcome sin in our thought life is to align our thoughts with God, who always sees us as righteous in Christ.

RE-ENVISION THE BATTLE

Putting to death the deeds of the body (8:13) is not about willpower, asceticism, or escaping our physicality. The difference between living by the flesh and living by the Spirit is about who or what we rely on—whether our own efforts or what God has done for us (see chapters 3–5). Crucifying the flesh means overruling sinfulness, laying aside the old way of life for the new.

Refuse to see your failures as cause for condemnation. For a believer, they never are. They are almost always an invitation to come closer, to lean on the Spirit, to ask persistently for his power, and to take your eyes off the failure (as difficult as that might be). It feels careless to ignore sin—it's human instinct to focus on the problem and want to fix it—but if the old self has died in Christ, ignoring it is the right thing do. Be wholly preoccupied with the Spirit, who freely gives you life and peace.

But you are not controlled by your sinful nature. You are controlled by the Spirit if you have the Spirit of God living in you. (And remember that those who do not have the Spirit of Christ living in them do not belong to him at all.) And Christ lives within you. . . . The Spirit of God, who raised Jesus from the dead, lives in you.

8:9-11

At several points in this letter, Paul has pointed to various stages on the spectrum of obedience (see comments and diagram on page 92). At one end is obedience *against* nature, described so personally in 7:14-25. It's a frustrating and futile existence because fallen humanity cannot live the unfallen life. At the other end is obedience *from* nature, described in 8:5-14, a picture of the new-humanity life that is fully restored (or being restored) into the image of God. Much of our lifelong discipleship is a matter of moving from one end of the spectrum to the other.

Many Christians spend a lifetime trying to train their old nature to obey—an arduous path of willpower and self-discipline that can reprogram our behavior to a degree but never really changes us from within. But as we've seen, the goal is not to learn to obey God against our nature—that's no different from law—even though there will be times when raw obedience is all we have. It's always better to obey a law, rule, principle, or precept than not. But this raw obedience signals a need for deeper transformation in that area. And we can only get it through the power of God's Spirit.

Open up to receive the Spirit—not just once but continuously. Ask him to breathe the life of God into you, to rearrange your thoughts, feelings, instincts, and impulses, to energize and empower you from within. In your mind's eye, *see* him responding. The more you cultivate that image—and know that it's much more than an image—the more you will sense his movement within. His voice and impressions may often sound like your own, but only because he is transforming you from within rather than speaking to you from the outside. Over time, you will learn to recognize when he is at work.

RE-ENVISION HIS PRESENCE

Relying on the Spirit is a new way of life, and it can seem discouragingly unfamiliar and ethereal to us when we're looking for evidence of inward change. For a more concrete image, envision Jesus' blood flowing through your veins, reconstituting your nature into a new, heavenly one. This involves a new way of thinking, as 6:1-14, 8:5-14, and 12:2 suggest—a reprogramming of our thoughts that transforms how we live. But it's more than just a cognitive-behavioral change; it also involves a reconstruction of our innermost being. The Spirit of Jesus—the same one who walked the land of promise two millennia ago and still springs off the pages of the Gospels—really is within us to energize and empower our lives. Your new nature is implanted within you, with plenty of room to grow. Rest in the Spirit God has given you and let him flourish in every inch of your being.

FROM SLAVES TO CHILDREN

All who are led by the Spirit of God are children of God. So you have not received a spirit that makes you fearful slaves. Instead, you received God's Spirit when he adopted you as his own children. Now we call him, "Abba, Father."

8:14-15

The first part of this chapter has been full of contrasts: the power of sin and the power of the Spirit (8:2), the law of Moses and the sacrifice of the Son (8:3-4), two radically different mindsets (8:5), and the way of the flesh and the way of the Spirit. Here the contrast is between slaves and children. We were once enslaved to sin (6:16), and even when we present ourselves as slaves to God (6:18, 22), he receives us as children and heirs. This is not just a transfer of loyalty or ownership. It's an adoption.

It's also an exodus from everything that once held us captive—a new exodus in the pattern of the old, a departure from sin's slavery into the glorious promise, with the Holy Spirit as the manifestation of God's presence.* It's clear throughout Romans what we have been set free *from* (that horrific condition of sin, futility, corruption, decay), and Paul has touched on what we've been set free *for* (a new life in the Spirit). But here the purpose of our freedom is further defined. We are set free for a family relationship, a deeper level of intimacy than

* N. T. Wright, *Paul: In Fresh Perspective* (Minneapolis: Fortress Press, 2005), 149. Wright finds parallels between Israel's experience of God's manifest presence and glory in the wilderness and Paul's descriptions of our deliverance from sin into freedom and the ultimate Promised Land in Romans.

we've ever experienced, a welcoming into our heart's true home. No longer is it about whether we've kept the law. It's about being united with God in a familial bond. That's why the gift of righteousness Paul has discussed at such length is so important. It recasts us in the image of our Father. We carry his spiritual DNA and reflect his nature as his children.

RE-ENVISION YOUR HOME

Many Christians come to God with the question, *What do you want me to do?* It's not a bad question, but it is far from the priority. The question we should be asking daily is, *Lord, who am I?* Or more specifically, *Who am I in relation to who you are?* Answer that one, and the *doing* becomes intuitive, natural, organic, and purposeful.

When it really sinks in that you're a son or daughter of God—that this *Abba* is your Daddy—everything changes. When you're visiting someone, you are never yourself, even when the host tells you to "make yourself at home." But sons and daughters don't have to be told to make themselves at home; they have the run of the place. That's your position in God's Kingdom, and you can freely enjoy all the privileges as a member of the royal family, now and forever.

HEIRS OF EVERYTHING

Since we are his children, we are his heirs. In fact, together with Christ we are heirs of God's glory.

8:17

Inheritance is a big deal to God. Numerous Old Testament laws safeguard the inheritance of God's people—their piece of the Promised Land—to ensure every family's share. Almost all of God's promises were intended to bless not only the generation that received them but also many generations to come. Even Abraham, the father of this faith we've been given, looked ahead to a multitude of descendants and a city built by God, though he died long before the promise could ever be fulfilled (Genesis 12:1-3; Hebrews 11:10, 13, 29-40). God transcends generations and wants each one to build on what has gone before and set the next one up for even more.

In the New Testament, Paul designates all believers, whether Jew or Gentile, as heirs of Abraham's promise (Galatians 3:29). But our inheritance goes further than that. Here (and in Galatians 4:7), he says we are also co-heirs with Christ. Since Jesus stands to inherit everything (Hebrews 1:2), we stand to inherit everything with him. Even now, the Son and his co-heirs are invited to ask for the nations of the earth as an inheritance (Psalm 2:8)—a critical invitation to take seriously if we are to fulfill our global mission.

Early in this letter, we were rebels worthy of condemnation. Now we're co-heirs of the entire Kingdom, wherever Jesus reigns, which will be everywhere and over everything. (He is already sovereign everywhere, but not much of this world has yet submitted to his reign, as is evident almost everywhere we look.) We come to find out that we will one day reign with him (Revelation 5:10), and in some respects we already do (1 Peter 2:9). We've gone from death to life, futility to fruitfulness, slavery to freedom, condemnation to a coronation. It's a glorious journey.

RE-ENVISION YOUR INHERITANCE

We were created to bear God's image, which includes not only his righteousness but also his glory. Paul recognized this calling in describing our transformation "from glory to glory" (2 Corinthians 3:18, NKJV, NASB). You'll notice in that passage that this transformation does not come from striving to do better or be Christlike. It comes from gazing at Jesus with unveiled faces. The Spirit enters into that face-to-face communion with abundant power to change.

As a royal heir of the Kingdom, see yourself as a bearer of God's glory (John 17:22), and spend far more time being fascinated with his goodness than trying to live up to it. The living will come, but not without the vision that empowers it. Like a young athlete mimicking his hero or an intern mentored by the CEO, you grow into the image you set before yourself daily. You are not only inheriting the Kingdom; you are also inheriting the nature of the King.

THE COST OF GLORY

If we are to share his glory, we must also share his suffering. Yet what we suffer now is nothing compared to the glory he will reveal to us later.

8:17-18

Paul's first missionary journey met with considerable success but also with considerable opposition. After he and Barnabas preached in several cities, they made a second pass through them on their way home. They appointed elders and prayed with each fledgling church, exhorting them with a reminder that "we must suffer many hardships to enter the Kingdom of God" (Acts 14:22). Apparently there's a cost to glory.

Paul would never have implied that we must suffer *in order* to enter the Kingdom, of course. That would contradict his entire message of salvation by grace through faith alone. But based on his own experience, he would insist that turning the world upside down with the message of Jesus, or even experiencing the Kingdom as fully as we should, will not be a smooth, easy process. Jesus told his disciples as much, assuring them that even though they would face trials and tribulations in this world, they should nevertheless rejoice because he had already overcome the world (John 16:33). Seeing in a radically new way and living out our new vision comes at a cost.

But we never have to worry that the cost will be greater than the benefits. Whatever we go through in life, however difficult, painful, and overwhelming it may feel at the time, it pales in comparison to the inheritance we will receive and the glory that comes with it. That's how glory works even in this world; people make enormous sacrifices to win a championship or achieve a dream. In the Kingdom, the stakes are infinitely higher, and though the suffering can feel excruciating and soul-crushing, it can never overshadow the beauty and brilliance of what's coming. Sharing Jesus' glory and sharing his suffering are part of the same package.

RE-ENVISION THE END

Imagine what it will be like in heaven one day. As you look back over your life in this fallen world, you'll recognize all the problems and pain you experienced, but you'll already know how everything turned out. From that vantage point, with the overwhelming glories of God's eternal Kingdom all around you and knowing you will enjoy them forever, your old life—which once looked so heavy and disheartening—will seem like a blip on the screen of eternity. All the worries you once had will be resolved. Though you could hardly see through them at the time, your steadfast faith will be rewarded. You may have even questioned whether all the pain was worth it, but on that day you'll know it was.

Blessed are those who can bring that future vision into the here and now. It doesn't eliminate the problems and pain, but it does strip them of power. When the suffering grows bigger in our minds than the glory does, we despair. When the glory grows bigger than the suffering, we endure with hope, peace, and perhaps even joy. Remember, your problems have an expiration date. Your glorious future does not. Fill your mind with a vision of the inheritance that never ends.

A REVELATION OF YOU

The creation waits in eager expectation for the children of God to be revealed.

8:19, NIV

From the depths of brokenness and futility, the world is crying out for God. Many people don't know that's the cry of their heart. They push God away because they think that if he's real at all, their heart could never be satisfied in him. But deep inside, that's every person's longing and what we were created for. And there's another longing that goes along with our longing for God and provides evidence that our deepest needs can be met after all. It's a revelation of God's children—those who know they are loved by him, filled with him, and joyfully satisfied in him. God's primary way of revealing himself is through his people.

As Paul expresses it, this "eager expectation" looks to the future for fulfillment, but there are present implications too. As he says, this creation has been groaning "up to the present time" (8:22). Paul does point to the distant future, but he may also be pointing to a more immediate need, as if to say, "All of creation is waiting for you to step into who you really are and show them what the new creation looks like." In other words, go ahead and be who you are in Christ. It's time.

This ongoing revelation of God's children—in part now, in full later—is vital. We often pray for an unmasking of evil—for the exposure of networks of drug trafficking, human trafficking, financial and political corruption, scams and frauds, and so on—but our prayers can't stop there. Unmasking evil would simply expose the problems; but without a simultaneous revelation of God's presence and power in those who love and serve him, it would create a crisis of cynicism and hopelessness. Many in the world may reject us, but many more need to know that God lives and works among us. As the "hands and feet" of Jesus, we play an indispensable role in pointing people to him.

RE-ENVISION YOUR PURPOSE

A revelation of the children of God may have many facets, but one of them is surely that we are called to live unexplainable lives that can only be attributed to God's power and presence. Notice that Paul doesn't say this groaning creation is eager for the Christian *message*—clearly it is not—but it *is* eager for Christ as he really is. The world is looking for a demonstration, not a doctrine. By faith, we can live supernaturally, demonstrate the heart of the Father, reflect his image (as apples who haven't fallen far from the tree), and display his presence in this world. A complete revelation of his children will come, but he is revealing us even now. See yourself as a crucial part of that revelation and live out your calling to the full.

CREATION'S LONGING

All creation has been groaning as in the pains of childbirth right up to the present time.

8:22

"The creation was subjected to futility" (8:20, ESV), not because God is vengeful but because he is compassionate. Our frustration and futility play an essential role in driving us in the direction of a Savior (8:21); we need to know something is wrong in order to turn to the one who can make things right. A prosperous life with no prospect of death or loss would create an illusion that all is well and God isn't needed. But in our brokenness and pain, we learn to long for something more.

That "something more" has been building throughout human existence as God's redemptive plan has unfolded. Like the pains of childbirth, full of both excitement and agony, the new creation has been birthed into this world and is still coming forth through those who believe. Jesus came in "the fullness of time" (Galatians 4:4, ESV); two millennia later, anticipation for ultimate fulfillment is still growing. Other religions have their opinions on the consummation of the age; we have within us the one who rules the ages.

That puts us in a fascinating position. Our world is subject to futility, yet we are heirs of a Kingdom that isn't, and for now we live in both. We face the challenges of navigating two realms simultaneously, and those two realms are often at odds with one another. Our calling is to bring incorruptible Kingdom life into earthly experience however we can. In fact, that's one of the ways God's children are unveiled. In as many ways as possible, we orient our faith, prayers, thoughts, words, and actions toward seeing God's will done on earth as it is in heaven (Matthew 6:10). We are to live as outposts of heaven in a fallen world, the human intersection of spiritual and material realms.

RE-ENVISION YOUR POSITION

You may not have thought of yourself as a connecting point between heaven and earth, but you are. Jesus showed us what that looks like (John 1:51; 5:19; 12:49-50) and calls us to follow his example (John 14:12-14; 20:21). We are his ambassadors (2 Corinthians 5:20)—and even more remarkably, his embassies, places where his Kingdom is made manifest. The world has been groaning with the agony of labor pains, not knowing the fulfillment to come. We live with excited anticipation of it and can even give people a glimpse of the unseen realm by making it visible in our lives. The foretaste of fulfillment in us—peace with God, the righteousness of Jesus, the power of the Spirit, and anything else that represents the environment of heaven—feeds the hunger of a world yearning for more.

OUR INTERPRETER

The Holy Spirit prays for us with groanings that cannot be expressed in words. And the Father who knows all hearts knows what the Spirit is saying, for the Spirit pleads for us believers in harmony with God's own will.

8:26-27

The power of the Spirit gives us life (8:11), prompts us to cry out to our Father as his beloved children (8:15), and gives us a foretaste of glory and our release from suffering (8:23). Each of these ministries of the Spirit demonstrates how profoundly he is working within us; but there is another ministry that is even more deeply personal. The Spirit helps us in our weakness by praying for us in groanings too profound for words. From the beginning of our faith to the fullness of all God has called us to experience, we are filled with, inspired by, and saturated in the Spirit's work.

We don't always feel that way, but we can take comfort in the fact that he is working within us even when we don't sense his presence. If we let him—and it often takes a conscious decision to do so—he inspires our thoughts, perspectives, and emotions; energizes us with spiritual power and perseverance; comforts and heals us; corrects us compassionately; and speaks words of wisdom and revelation to us. He is the power working within us by which God does infinitely more than we can ask or think (Ephesians 3:20). For people well acquainted with weakness (Romans 8:26), that's profoundly encouraging.

This is why we don't need to worry about coming up with the right words when we pray. God is not dependent on human language; we can present to him mental pictures, inexpressible needs, and vague desires for his intervention. As intercessors for the inexpressible needs of fallen humanity, we can groan and grieve with God's Spirit—like creation does in 8:22 and Paul in 9:2-3. Yes, it helps to pray specifically when we can, but sometimes we can't. No matter. The Spirit takes what is indescribable for us and translates it into divine language. Most servants have to learn the protocol and rhetoric of petitioning a king, but we are more than servants. We are the King's children. The cry of our hearts is enough.

RE-ENVISION YOUR PRAYERS

Perhaps you've envisioned prayer as simply a conversation between you and God. And at its core, it is. But divine participation in our prayers is much more involved than that. We can assume that many of our prayers are inspired by the Father's revealed will and the Spirit who works within us, but a lot more happens between our praying and God's hearing. The Spirit interprets and intercedes with groanings too deep for words, the Son intercedes and advocates for us (8:34; Hebrews 7:25), and the Father hears and answers (Matthew 7:7-11; 1 John 5:14-15). Our requests are not a shot in the dark; they are inspired and guided, accompanied by God's presence, purpose, and power from beginning to end. Always enter into the fullness of that conversation as a participant in the divine council, with confidence and faith.

THE STORY OF OUR LIVES

We know that God causes everything to work together for the good of those who love God and are called according to his purpose for them.

8:28

Having just read about this groaning world and suffering believers (8:17, 22), we might wonder how thoroughly we've escaped the futility of creation. We know creation will one day be freed from death and decay (8:21), but until it is, can we really be sure that God's will is being accomplished in our lives? After all, even as believers, we still experience frustration and futility at times. We've done things that do not fit God's purposes for us, and it would be reasonable to think that the potential for fulfilling those purposes has been compromised. Though we've been saved from this fallen world, we know its fallenness still affects us.

The context for 8:28 is the Spirit's ministry of intercession within us and on our behalf. Our prayers are entirely in the Spirit's and the Father's hands (and as we will soon see in 8:34, also in the hands of Jesus). But Paul makes it clear that our circumstances, relationships, good decisions, bad decisions—"everything," as mentioned in 8:28—are in God's hands too. This is not fate or a series of happy coincidences. God sovereignly orchestrates the elements of our lives, accounting for even tragic events or misguided choices ahead of time, to bring about the best outcomes for his purposes and our well-being. He steers our stories toward good ends.

Scripture is full of examples of redeemed dysfunction, even from its earliest pages. The patriarchal families of Abraham, Isaac, Jacob, and Joseph were marked with fears, doubts, deception, competitive childbearing, grudges, violence, and betrayal, even as they lived under a covenant that established Israel as God's chosen people. The journey to the Promised Land under Moses and then Joshua included rebellion, faithlessness, and long delays that God had prefigured into his timing. David's ascent to the throne as the king with a messianic legacy involved exile and infighting, and his reign was scarred by adultery and murder, yet the son of a marriage that never should have happened built the Temple, authored Scripture, and oversaw the golden age of the kingdom. God has an amazing track record of bringing good out of very flawed people and disastrous circumstances. He foresees all our traumas, tragedies, dysfunctional messes, mistakes, and missteps, and he masterfully integrates them into his plan for his purposes and our good.

RE-ENVISION YOUR PAST

It's easy to live with regret, but as children of the God who redeems the traumas and tragedies of our lives—even the self-inflicted ones—we don't have to. God does not promise that everything will work out perfectly—it's possible to miss a calling or forfeit a promise through unbelief—but he always has a way to bring us back into his purposes and demonstrate his goodness. No matter what we've been through, he blesses those who love him.

You may look back over your life and lament, *Look at what I've missed!* God looks at your life and says, *Look at what you've overcome!* A true view of his sovereign redemption turns your failures into victories, your losses into gains, your emptiness into fullness, your brokenness into restoration. The things you regret are the things you will forever celebrate as part of your redemption story.

OUR PURPOSE FULFILLED

God knew his people in advance, and he chose them to become like his Son, so that his Son would be the firstborn among many brothers and sisters. . . . And having given them right standing, he gave them his glory.

8:29-30

God is able to work out his purposes in everything (8:28) because he sees everything in advance. With that foreknowledge, he decides in advance how to accomplish his will. He doesn't manipulate us by pulling the strings of our lives and inflicting hardships on us—the fallen world we live in occasions those hardships quite effectively—but he does preordain his purposes for us. And his greatest purpose is for us to become like his Son, the perfect image of the Father (Colossians 1:15; Hebrews 1:3), in fulfillment of the image we were given at creation. From falling short of glory (Romans 3:23), we now hope in it (5:2), have it revealed in us (8:18), and share in it fully (8:30).

No one disputes that predestination is biblical—the concept occurs in this passage (and in 1 Corinthians 2:7; Ephesians 1:5, 11)—but what it implies is widely debated. Even so, we can agree on God's ultimate intent for everyone he calls. We are being restored into the divine image, birthed through the power of a new genesis, endowed with the glory God gives us to reflect him well. We may have been told that God wants us to "be like Jesus"—an impossible burden if we don't know all it entails—but the fullness of that image is all we could have hoped for and more. It includes his presence, power, purposes, promises, and perfection. We become brothers and sisters of the King.

We have no reason to worry—God's purposes will be accomplished in the lives of his people. The previous verse assured us that they will. From beginning to end, our comprehensive salvation is in his hands. The law keepers Paul wrote about earlier did not have that assurance. Those who rest in the salvation Jesus accomplished for us do. This is where grace that comes by faith and the Spirit's intercession will lead us.

RE-ENVISION YOUR DESTINY

Many Christians see the call to be Christlike as a behavioral issue. But acting like Jesus is a futile role to play if we aren't inwardly becoming like him. This is not about something we do; it's about who we are—and not who we *think* we are but who God *says* we are. We have to fully embrace the identity of Jesus within us if we are going to grow into the image he has given us.

Children don't try to take on the image of their parents. They just do. Neither do they obsess about behavioral outcomes. They simply act according to the nature and nurture they are given. Our adult tendency to focus on outcomes can lead to a discipleship that is all willpower and self-discipline, but real change is a matter of input. If we enter into deep fellowship with God, cultivate our love for him, and allow ourselves to be amazed by his nature, character, and glory, we will be changed from the inside out. And we will begin to look a lot like Jesus.

ON OUR SIDE

If God is for us, who can ever be against us? Since he did not spare even his own Son but gave him up for us all, won't he also give us everything else?

8:31-32

God is on our side. We often insist that it should be the other way around—that in a God-centered life, we need to be on his side rather than assume that he is there to serve us—and Scripture clearly affirms that perspective. But it also tells us that God is for us (see also Psalm 118:6; 124:1-2). For everyone who has wondered whether God really wants to answer our prayers, if he loves us because he has to and not because he actually has any affection for us, or if he fills our lives with hardship because we need so much correction, this is good news. He has demonstrated how strongly he loves, upholds, defends, protects, and provides for us by giving up his own Son for us. Why, after showing us such enormous generosity, would he start withholding things now?

Paul has filled this passage with evidence of God's favor. God has freed us from the power of sin and death (8:1-13); he has made us his children and heirs (8:14-17); he has promised us glory and new bodies (8:18-25); the Holy Spirit prays for us and through us (8:26-27); God works in all things on our behalf, and through us for our good and his glory (8:28-30); he has given us his Son and "everything else" (8:31-32); Jesus himself is interceding for us (8:34); and we can never be separated from the love of God and Christ, through whom we have overwhelming victory (8:35-39). What more could we want?

Yet for children of an invincible God who has clearly shown us his favor, we far too easily give in to a defeatist attitude. Perhaps we are overly focused on the circumstances we face, or maybe we just forget how extravagant God's gifts and promises are. No matter how astonishing our eternity is, our here and now can be difficult. That's why Paul aims to elevate the vision of these Romans—and why, two millennia later, we should expand our vision too.

RE-ENVISION YOUR STANDING

To help us envision our standing, Paul uses courtroom language of accusation and condemnation in the next two verses (8:33-34), echoing his declaration at the beginning of the chapter that there is no condemnation for those who are in Christ. If we were accused of a crime and had no way to refute the evidence against us, we would expect a guilty verdict and lose hope. But when we realize that our Father is the judge, our brother is the defense attorney, and the prosecutor has no credibility, the whole scenario swings dramatically in our favor. God is on our side. A guilty verdict isn't even in the picture. A joyful, fulfilling future is assured.

Live all of life with that perspective. Refuse to see it as a distant hope obscured by today's challenges. Embrace the joy of it now and expect God to give you everything for a "rich and satisfying life" (John 10:10).

OVERWHELMING OVERCOMING

Can anything ever separate us from Christ's love? . . . No, despite all these things, overwhelming victory is ours through Christ, who loved us.

8:35, 37

The implicit message of Romans 8 up to this point is that, by virtue of our position in Christ, a gift of God's grace and received by faith, our own sins and mistakes have no bearing on our standing in Christ or God's overwhelming love for us. We are righteous, free, accepted, understood, empowered, favored, and blessed. Our sinfulness—including the guilt and shame that accompanied it—will never separate us from Jesus.

Neither will anything else. Not even extreme circumstances such as calamity, persecution, hunger, destitution, danger, or death can interrupt our relationship with God. He may correct us and discipline us, but he will never cease to love us and work for our good. Though some people grow disillusioned through hardships and pain, we have every reason to draw close to the Lord through those experiences. In fact, they create a platform for him to demonstrate his overwhelming victory in us. We are "more than conquerors" through them (8:37, NIV, ESV, NKJV).

We therefore have no reason to live as defeatists in this overwhelmingly victorious Kingdom. Our well-being is not subject to circumstances. In fact, circumstances are subject to us—or rather Christ in us. We are not sheltered from all persecution and pain; rather we follow the path walked by Jesus

(Isaiah 53:3-10), Paul (2 Corinthians 4:8-10), and many others who have felt like sheep for slaughter (Romans 8:36, quoting Psalm 44:22). But just as Jesus' suffering and death led to resurrection and glory, ours does too (8:17-18). In all of life's battles, we have the upper hand.

RE-ENVISION YOUR VICTORY

Many believers associate pain and hardship with God's disfavor. But God favors us in the midst of it all. Even calamity, persecution, hunger, destitution, danger, and death have no power to separate us from his love and make no statement on our relationship with him. They do not serve as evidence that we are out of his will, lacking enough faith, or walking without God-given authority. They are simply the context in which his love and our faith are proved.

Refuse to see your journey of faith as a defensive battle. You aren't just equipped to survive. You are empowered to thrive, even in crises and conflict. In Christ, you have the upper hand and the assurance of overwhelming victory in all of life's challenges. Your Savior is more than a conqueror of sin, death, and all the ravages of the old humanity. In him, so are you.

ROMANS 9–11

HAS GOD TAKEN BACK HIS PROMISES?

If God's covenant with Israel is now open to Gentiles—and without Gentiles having to buy in to all the Torah's requirements—does that mean God has rejected Israel and chosen the largely Gentile church to replace it? Has he reneged on his promises? After centuries of expressing his love and faithfulness to Israel (as well as his warnings and corrections), has he brushed them off with a "never mind"? Has the betrothal at Sinai (Jeremiah 2:2; Ezekiel 16:8, 60) ended in a divorce?

Chapters 9–11 are Paul's resounding *no* to all these questions. He argues that this turning away of Israel (with exceptions, including Paul and other Jewish believers) and the concurrent acceptance of Gentiles is no accident of history, or—from God's perspective—an unexpected turn of events (9:6-29). Abraham and his descendants were vehicles of the solution to humanity's crisis but not the solution itself or the end goal. They were, like Gentiles, among the old humanity but were chosen as the context in which God would reveal the new humanity. The law had to highlight sin in someone, and that someone was Israel, blessed to receive the covenant but the recipient of its judgments as well. Presented with life and prosperity or death and destruction (Deuteronomy 30:12-15), fallen humanity could long for the former but only reap the latter. But Israel also became the context for the law's fulfillment in Jesus. As Paul shows in chapter 10, the Messiah reveals what had been God's plan all along.

What happens to Israel now? Are there two kinds of chosen people, each with a separate track to salvation? Not at all. The root of the covenant has remained the same, but some branches are being broken off and others grafted in (11:16-24). And even if the majority of Israel was being broken off in Paul's day, a day is coming when Israel will recognize its Messiah and return to the covenant (11:12, 24, 26). God's wisdom in drawing the world to himself through one people, then many, and then blessing all by fulfilling his promises to all, is unfathomable and full of glory (11:33-36).

BACKGROUND

If Romans is an overview of salvation theology, chapters 9–11 are a long parenthetical interlude. If Romans is a theodicy—a justification of God's works that on the surface may appear to be unjustified—then chapters 9–11 are the apex. If Romans is an effort to mend relationships between Jews and Gentiles in the churches of Rome, chapters 9–11 fit into the flow of the argument as an explanation of why Jewishness is still relevant in God's Kingdom (per 3:1-2). Looking at the letter through each of these lenses highlights different truths, all with some justification—unless they lead to a conclusion that Israel is marginal to salvation history. In Paul's mind, salvation history cannot be understood apart from God's covenant with Israel.

In these chapters, he envisions the metanarrative of God's plan—the huge shifts involved in choosing a single people, revealing himself through that people, bringing his revelation to a climactic completion, and then launching the message of that revelation to the whole world—all while maintaining his special relationship with the original chosen people and making it clear that others are chosen too.

This section of the letter addresses any Gentiles in the Roman church who might have thought that God's promises to the Jews had now been taken from them and passed on to the Gentiles instead—i.e., that Gentile believers had replaced Israel. In light of the expulsion of Jews from Rome in AD 49 and their perhaps unpopular return in the mid-50s, the idea of Jews being shut out of God's plan might have seemed appealing to some. But this is not so. Gentile believers have been grafted into Israel by faith, even as many (but not all) Jews have been cut off for not believing. But it's still the same tree, and those Jews can be grafted back in. In fact, this is by God's design, as Israel will experience a resurrection of its own—seemingly cast off (11:15) but with hope of its people returning to life through faith in the covenant of their own Messiah.

This passage also addresses those Jews who are alarmed by the kind of statements Paul makes in 2:29; 3:9; and Galatians 3:28—that there is no longer any distinction between Greek and Jew in Christ—and who don't want to give up their Jewishness. The idea that our identity is now formed by a belief rather than an ethnicity or a tradition was a hard sell in the ancient world, though Jews were already further along than most on this point, seeing themselves as heirs of a covenant rather than simply of a culture. Still, their "exclusive" relationship with God was now enormously and uncomfortably inclusive. God was never redeeming only Israel; his plan was also to redeem the world.

THE BIG PICTURE

Centuries earlier, the prophet Jeremiah repeatedly warned that judgment was coming, but most Jews thought he was overreacting to the nation's problems. God would never allow his chosen people to be defeated by violent, idolatrous Babylonians, they assumed. Other prophecies foretold numerous blessings on Jerusalem and its people. The city would become "the pride of the earth" (Isaiah 62:7), and the mountain of the Lord would be the highest and most important place in the world (Isaiah 2:2). Yet Jeremiah warned that the city would be destroyed. *Impossible*, they thought, and they were stunned when the Babylonian army besieged the city and walls began to fall.

The blessings and curses in Deuteronomy 28 capture both the incredible privilege and enormous responsibilities of being God's chosen people. The blessings were amazingly beautiful; the consequences of disregarding the covenant were devastating. Such a high calling could result in glory or utter disaster—life and prosperity or death and destruction (Deuteronomy 30:15-18). And because God's chosen people still carried Adam's sin-saturated nature, only one outcome was truly possible.

A calling from God is a weighty responsibility filled with both pain and promise, as Paul's passionate words in Romans 9–11 so compellingly affirm. But unlike ancient Israel, which could only strive to carry out this calling in the old nature of their fallen humanity, Jesus fulfilled it as the perfect image-bearer of God. His Spirit now plants that image-bearing nature in all who believe. Just as the law accomplished its work by exposing the futility of old humanity, the Spirit accomplishes his work by birthing a new humanity to renew and restore creation. And this powerful work turns history in a surprising new direction.

UNEXPECTED TURNS

My heart is filled with bitter sorrow and unending grief for my people, my Jewish brothers and sisters. I would be willing to be forever cursed—cut off from Christ!—if that would save them.

9:2-3

Chapter 8 is the pinnacle of Paul's letter, the great unfolding of the implications of living by grace through faith in Christ. It points to manifold blessings and promises, the present power and future hope, the invincibility of those who are firmly rooted in the love of Christ. This is the extraordinary new life given to Gentile and Jewish believers alike.

But if that's true, what about Israel? These have been God's chosen people, bearers of his covenants and law, stewards of the promises, the people through whom Jesus came (9:4-5). What can we say of these people to whom the law was given? If salvation is by grace through faith, going all the way back to Abraham, how are we to understand their covenant of law, which God promised would bring life to those who obey it wholeheartedly (10:5; Leviticus 18:5)? Has God's plan taken an unexpected turn?

Paul will get to that, but first he expresses deep grief that most of his compatriots have chosen to remain fixed on earlier revelation without moving with God as he revealed even more. God developed this covenant further, renewing it entirely by sending Jesus to fulfill the law, yet most Jews didn't track with this development. In fact, many who were aware of Paul's ministry among Gentiles questioned his loyalties. So he openly displays them here. He would trade places with his "Jewish brothers and sisters" if by missing out on the covenant he could lead them into it.

Modern Westerners are sometimes puzzled at this sense of solidarity, just as ancient people might be perplexed at our individualism. Many ancients saw themselves more corporately than individually, connected to a people as a whole and, in the case of Jews, to a divinely authored historical narrative. Paul seemed more concerned with the fate of his people than with his personal destiny, even while considering his own relationship with Christ a priceless treasure (Philippians 3:8-9). God continued to lead, but Paul's "brothers and sisters" stopped following, causing him "unending grief."

RE-ENVISION REVIVAL

The rejection of Jesus by Jews was a stunning turn of events from a human perspective, but it fits a long pattern. Revivals, renewals, reformations, and other prophetic movements often provoke opposition among entrenched traditionalists. Those involved in powerful moves of God try to capture and consolidate them by institutionalizing them—to preserve what God is doing—yet the institutions eventually grow stagnant as people cry out for a new move of God again. The guardians of the past are highly skeptical and critical of new movements, yet the Holy Spirit specializes in them—and is grieved when resisters miss what he is doing.

Don't get so stuck in where God has been that you miss where he is going. No, he's not going to give new revelation, but he does give new understanding and inspire new expressions. Honor how he moved yesterday, but be sensitive to how he is moving today. And be comfortable with unexpected turns.

THE FAMILY OF FAITH

Has God failed to fulfill his promise to Israel? No, for not all who are born into the nation of Israel are truly members of God's people! Being descendants of Abraham doesn't make them truly Abraham's children.

9:6-7

Abraham was promised a son, and he ended up with many (Genesis 16:15; 21:1-5; 25:1-6). But Isaac was the promised one, and only his descendants were heirs of the covenant. Only one of Isaac's sons carried that covenant forward (Romans 9:10-13); before Jacob and Esau were born, God said the older (Esau) would serve the younger (Jacob). Paul's point is that this covenant depended on God, who gave it, rather than on the people who received it. God made these choices apart from human intervention (8:29-30) and continues to carry out his purposes as he pleases.

God's promises haven't failed. In fact, he still sees both Israel and its promises as completely intact. But he defines Israel not according to flesh, inheritance, or ritual but rather according to faith (2:29; 3:9-12). Whether someone carries DNA that can be traced back to Abraham is irrelevant. What matters is whether they have Abraham's faith.

Many Jews would have agreed with this in principle. After all, they considered Rahab of Jericho, Ruth the Moabite, and Uriah the Hittite among their own. Israel had God-given ways of accepting foreigners—*if* those foreigners accepted their laws, traditions, and culture. Paul insists here that not only can foreigners become Jews at heart by faith apart from law, but Jews can become like foreigners if they reject God's purposes. So his answer to the question of whether God had rejected Israel is a resounding *no*. It was Israelites who had rejected God.

Certainly not all Jews fit that description, neither in Paul's day nor in ours. Nowhere does the New Testament say God is done with Israel or has rejected the Jews. It simply affirms salvation by grace through faith apart from the law, a Gentile-friendly message that offended many first-century Jews and led to a growing separation between natural and spiritual descendants of Abraham. Through that message, we are painted into the vast family portrait of God's people across the ages.

RE-ENVISION THE FAMILY PORTRAIT

By faith, you are an heir of God's promises regardless of your background—even if you were once far from the family of faith. Picture yourself in that family portrait, no matter how foreign it might feel at first. Resist the temptation to see God's promises to an ancient people as confined to a narrow context and off limits to you. Some promises were specific to a time and place; all reveal something about the nature and character of God and serve as invitations for you to experience him fully. Accept that invitation eagerly, and often, as an heir of all he has promised.

A CHOSEN MERCY

God chooses people according to his own purposes; he calls people, but not according to their good or bad works. . . . It is God who decides to show mercy. We can neither choose it nor work for it.

9:11-12, 16

God knows all things in advance—it's how Jesus was slain before the world was made (Revelation 13:8) and how God records all our days before they happen (Psalm 139:16)—but Paul describes something much deeper than foreknowledge here. God isn't just prophesying lives like Jacob's and Esau's ahead of time and letting them play out. He's directing the show.

Is this fair? If God can choose to give mercy to whomever he wants and soften or harden hearts however he wants (as Paul asserts in his quoting of Exodus 9:12, 16; 33:19), isn't he unilaterally determining who will receive his mercy and respond to his promises? If he chooses people like Isaac and Jacob as heirs of the covenant and also ordains that people like Pharaoh will harden their hearts to him (Romans 9:17-18), who's to blame for anything? An even more uncomfortable question for Paul's readers is whether it was fair for God to choose Israel as his firstborn nation and declare his faithfulness to them for centuries, knowing they would end up rejecting the Messiah he gave them. Was he just using them? If it's all God's choice and no human decisions or works are involved, is God's justice really just?

These questions have been debated for centuries, with some theologians emphasizing God's sovereign election and our dependence on him to even respond in faith, and other theologians emphasizing God's foreknowledge of human choices while respecting free will. Biblical revelation is deep and wide enough to encourage varying interpretations and perspectives. Paul's point here is that both Jewish and Gentile responses to the gospel fit God's purposes. What seemed from the perspective of Jewish believers like Paul to be a disastrous turn of events for Israel was not a crisis from God's perspective. Surely God grieved with Paul over Jewish rejection of the Messiah, but it did not fall outside his redemptive plan.

RE-ENVISION SOVEREIGNTY

Perhaps you've felt the tension between different outlooks on life. Is it predetermined fate, a random free-for-all, or something in between? Are things *meant* to happen or do they just happen? Does our future depend on God, on us, or some of both? Where does the Christian life fit on this spectrum of determinism?

Parsing the distinctions between God's will, what he has allowed in a fallen world, and the works of our spiritual adversary is always tricky and sometimes too complex for definition. But if it seems that the world, the church, or your own life is out of control, be encouraged by God's sovereignty as it is revealed here and elsewhere in Scripture. When we don't see the end of the story, we may give in to fear, disappointment, discouragement, or anger. God does see the end of it and promises that it's good for those who love him—even for the many who do not love him now but eventually will. In one way or another, his mercy stands behind everything we face, and it's a mercy he has gladly chosen to give.

IN THE POTTER'S HANDS

Should the thing that was created say to the one who created it, "Why have you made me like this?"

9:20

God told Jeremiah to go watch a potter, and when the prophet saw the potter crush a half-molded pot back into a lump of clay and start over, God said he could do the same with nations as he pleases (see Jeremiah 18:1-11). History is full of nations that have risen and fallen under God's sovereign hand, and Paul points out that the nation of Israel is one of them. God can bless or withhold blessing however he chooses.

Paul would also have been well acquainted with the Wisdom of Solomon, a book in the Greek translation of the Old Testament (the Septuagint), in which a potter makes some vessels for good and clean uses, and others for unclean or dishonorable uses (Wisdom 15:7). Paul's point in reiterating this theme is that God has his purposes in how he has dealt with the Jewish people, and no complaints that he has been unfair are justified.

We often debate whether God bases his judgments on his foreknowledge of our choices and beliefs or more directly determines those choices and beliefs. Paul doesn't directly answer that question, though he clearly defends God's judgments. The bigger issue, according to Paul, is God's right to treat his own creation however he wants. His statement that some vessels are "destined for destruction" (9:22) seems especially harsh, though no harsher than the statements of the Old Testament prophets. Even so, this is less about God's wrath than his purposes. The real issue is his plan for revealing and demonstrating his nature and character through the rise and fall of peoples and their responses to him. As the sovereign Creator, he has his reasons for this plan, even if many aspects of it remain a mystery to us.

RE-ENVISION USEFULNESS

Avoid the temptation to see yourself as a tool being used by God, some inanimate vessel made simply to serve his purposes. Nowhere does Scripture portray those who faithfully love and serve God in such utilitarian terms. We are Jesus' friends (John 15:15), his bride (2 Corinthians 11:2; Revelation 21:2), and God's children (Romans 8:15-16; John 1:12; Galatians 4:6), all deeply personal and affectionate portrayals. You are God's beloved.

But when you look at the rise and fall of nations and the vitriol of those who reject God, Paul's image of the potter and his clay explains a lot. This is the way to see history under the hand of a sovereign God. We live in a world that seems to be in chaos but is really serving to display who God is. And as his beloved, we are part of the most gratifying side of that display. We become demonstrations of his faithfulness, kindness, and mercy toward those who believe.

WHERE GLORY SHINES

He does this to make the riches of his glory shine even brighter on those to whom he shows mercy, who were prepared in advance for glory.

9:23

We love God for his amazing attributes. He is all-knowing, all-powerful, and ever-present. His central attribute is love, and he demonstrates it in a multitude of ways. But we also love God for his healing, deliverance, protection, comfort, and mercy, hardly realizing that these characteristics would have remained forever hidden to the human race and angelic observers if we had never fallen.

Think about that. God cannot heal unless someone is sick, deliver unless someone is captive, protect unless there are dangers, comfort in the absence of pain, or forgive when no wrongs have been committed. All these attributes require a context of fallenness, and God could never have revealed himself this fully in a perfect world. More specifically, he could not reveal himself *through his people* if we did not live in this kind of world.

That's a high price to pay for glory, yet as Paul has already said, our present sufferings cannot compare to the glory that will be and is already being revealed (8:18; 2 Corinthians 4:17). God has chosen to reveal glory and even impart it to those who love him—who, astonishingly to some first-century Jews, include Gentiles, as Paul makes clear in his quotes from Old Testament texts (9:25-26). This was always part of God's plan. For the fullness of revelation he desired, this is how it had to happen.

RE-ENVISION GOD'S PURPOSES

When it sinks into our hearts that human life in a fallen world is a platform for the revelation of God's glory—especially those attributes that cannot be displayed when all is well—our perspective on our adversity, problems, flaws, and weaknesses changes. These so-called crises are not getting in the way of God's work in our lives; they are the occasion for it. He wants to demonstrate who he is in the context of our trials and challenges.

That understanding turns every "why me?" into an entirely different line of questioning: "Lord, what do you want to do in this situation? How do you want to show yourself?" He will undoubtedly show you something—a healing or deliverance, provision or protection, or maybe even comfort and faithfulness to carry you through. However he shows himself, the revelation is good for you and those around you. This is how he revealed himself on the grand stage of human history with Jews and Gentiles, and it's how he reveals himself on the smaller yet still vitally significant stage of your life. Let him. He has always wanted the riches of his glory to shine brightly on you.

LIVING UNOFFENDED

They stumbled over the great rock in their path.

9:32

Many throughout Christian history have wrestled with Paul's words in this chapter. Though he presents Jesus as a stumbling block, his own argument is something of a stumbling block for countless readers. One reason for that is our individualistic reading of such passages, which sees every reference to God's rejection or acceptance in terms of our own salvation—as if God arbitrarily chooses whom to save (or not). Whatever truth there might be to that view, this particular passage may not even address our eternal destiny. Paul seems much more focused here on Israelites and Gentiles collectively, not as individuals.

In any case, he is certainly not making any sweeping statements about all Jews or all Gentiles, as he knows some from each group who have believed in Jesus and many more who have not. Just as certainly, he is not making any statements about Gentiles replacing Jews in God's plan; the first few chapters of this letter and the next two make that clear. God has great plans for both Jews and Gentiles, and movements of faith among them have been designed to maximize his glory and humanity's salvation. It will all end with people who come from different backgrounds but are all one in Christ.

Still, the unexpected turns in God's grand narrative caused many of Paul's fellow Jews to stumble. They had invested their entire lives in their calling as God's people, believing themselves to be the first (or only) examples of restored humanity. That calling was oriented around a covenant with Abraham and a law given through Moses. Now, in light of the mission to the Gentiles, those bedrock foundations didn't seem as firm as once thought.

God's plan often provokes resistance when it doesn't look like we expect it to. Jews—and even many Jewish believers in Jesus—felt disoriented by the Gentile mission. We, too, feel disoriented whenever God saves, restores, and empowers "unlikely" people. He works in surprising ways. Some people marvel at them. Others take offense.

RE-ENVISION GOD'S WAYS

Whatever it takes, learn to be unoffendable by God's ways. His Word is always true, and he will always keep his promises to you, but don't be surprised if he reorients your understanding of his Word or stretches your expectations in fulfilling those promises. God's people have a long history of predicting his plans and being entirely wrong about them. In all your expectations of how God works, cling to this one resolutely: that your journey with him will always be an adventure.

ZEAL AND TRUTH

I know what enthusiasm they have for God, but it is misdirected zeal. For they don't understand God's way of making people right with himself.

10:2-3

Paul knew all about misdirected zeal. He had lived that life as he pursued members of the new Jesus movement—seeking to bring them back to their senses, even if it meant bringing them to death. He was zealous about being right with God, defending God's purposes and his people from distortions like this strange Jesus movement, and upholding Jewish heritage and history as he understood it. But as he learned when he encountered the risen Jesus, Paul had been zealous about the wrong things.

Even as a follower of Jesus, he would never claim that the law was bad (see 7:12). The problem was that it can't empower us. It holds us to an ideal we can't achieve. The ideal is good, but it can only look down on us as we fall short. We can't embody the glory of God unless we're transformed by something much more powerful than the external Word.

Jesus changed everything. "Christ is the end of the law for righteousness to everyone who believes (10:4, ESV)—the "end" being the ultimate goal, the finished product, not the "end of its existence." According to Scripture, God's law is everlasting, and Jesus himself said it would not pass away until all is fulfilled. Then he fulfilled it.

This is not just a matter of law, grace, and faith. This is a matter of being set in our ways, fixed in our understanding, never allowing the possibility that God might rearrange our thinking. Paul was looking at a generation of people who had committed themselves to God and were trying to live out his ways faithfully. Yet they were missing the point. They were so focused on their own understanding that they couldn't see God at work right in front of them. Like many in Israel's history, they honored prophets from centuries past but rejected prophets in their own generation.

Many Christians have followed the same tradition. Many of the reformers and new movements we honor and respect today were attacked and vilified in their own time simply because they were new. Zeal for God without spiritual sensitivity to his ways is a universal problem.

It's important to have certain nonnegotiable anchor points. But anyone who believes their branch of Christianity has the full truth and that no other branch has anything important to offer has misunderstood the body of Christ and overestimated their own interpretations of Scripture. Like the religious experts of Jesus' day and the adherents of other religions (or no religion) do when they look at Jesus and Christians today, they set themselves up for stumbling blocks.

RE-ENVISION THE JOURNEY

Some Christians treat their beliefs as a stone structure. People may step in and out of their fortress, but none of their assumptions are open to discussion. Others see their beliefs as a journey to the eternal city. The city isn't going to change, but there are adventures to experience along the way, and they know they sometimes may be led on a route they didn't plan.

Keep your destination in full view, and never let it change. But be flexible on how God gets you there. Direct your zeal toward him alone, and follow however he leads.

SCRIPTURE AS DEFINITION OR INVITATION?

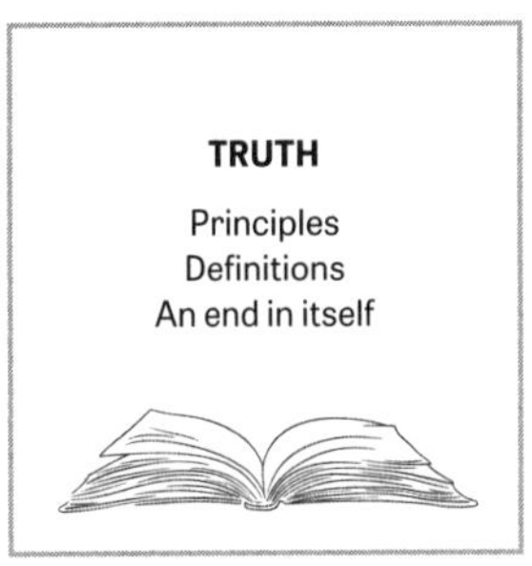

The Bible as religious text

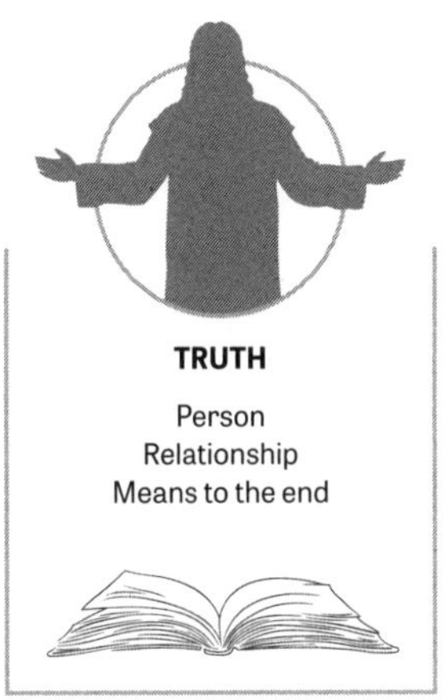

The Bible as relational gateway

In reality, the Bible is both defining and inviting, but a religious mindset often removes the personal element and turns it into an exclusive system of truth. Paul's description of first-century Jews' relationship to the law and their own covenant history suggests they were zealous for the principles, precepts, and standards God had given them without being sensitive to the person behind them. Christianity unquestionably has its own version of this mindset, and countless Christians slip unconsciously into a perspective that embraces intellectual understanding and principles but may close their minds to what God is doing here and now.

Scripture is more than a self-contained definer of our faith, and it is not our Savior. It's a gateway into a dynamic relationship with God that requires spiritual sensitivity, an open heart, and a willingness to be led, stretched, and transformed.

A MATTER OF THE HEART

Moses writes that the law's way of making a person right with God requires obedience to all of its commands.

10:5

The law is not too difficult to keep, said Moses. It is not kept in an unreachable heaven or across an impassable sea. It is readily at hand and presents a choice between a prosperous life and the destruction of death (Deuteronomy 30:11-16). In fact, all the blessings and curses of Deuteronomy 28 hinged on people's ability to keep this law—and, as Hebrew Scripture amply attests, Israel fell short of it for centuries and suffered the consequences.

In this passage, Paul refers to those verses, as well as to God's promise in Leviticus 18:5 that those who obey his decrees will find life in them. We often say similar things about God's instructions—that he only gives them for our good, and obeying them works out well for us. We can hardly condemn the concept in the law, especially since it came from God's own voice. And it's true—the law *would* have led to life if it empowered people to fulfill it. But because of the gap between fallen humanity and our original design, our efforts could never restore us or recapture our relationship with God. Only the works of a righteous man could fulfill a righteous law.

This conundrum points us back to the issue of obedience and our motives behind it. Do we obey God because we mistrust the Spirit within us and depend on instructions and principles? Or do we obey because we love him and trust what he has spoken and placed within us? One approach reflects self-sufficiency and ends in failure; the other reflects faith and a personal relationship. Few can discern this distinction in themselves, but it's a significant one. Even in a New Testament context, it's the difference between law and grace.

We'd be mistaken to assume that the Old Testament and Judaism are only about works and that Christians have ceased to rely on them. Many Jews obeyed God but trusted his mercy when they failed. The Old Testament emphasizes faith too, as Paul has noted, and many Christians emphasize grace but still try to earn God's favor. If we're looking for a distinction, it isn't between the two testaments. It's between the motives of the heart, and only God knows our true intent.

RE-ENVISION YOUR APPROACH

Are you striving for faith as Israel strived for the law? It won't work. Faith isn't something you can strive for; you simply receive it. It's right there, ready for your heart to embrace and your mouth to confess. It isn't a matter of pressing ahead for it. You lean back into it. It's based on what God has already accomplished. It's right to press forward for some things in the Kingdom—see Philippians 3:12-16, for example—but receiving salvation by grace through faith isn't one of them. Enter into your rest (Hebrews 4:1-11) and believe.

If you openly declare that Jesus is Lord and believe in your heart that God raised him from the dead, you will be saved. For it is by believing in your heart that you are made right with God, and it is by openly declaring your faith that you are saved.

10:9-10

These verses have been widely used evangelistically for centuries because they make for a concise summary of the salvation message. This is how we enter into the Kingdom. This evangelistic usage is not inappropriate, but there's more going on in these words than merely a call to faith. Paul specifically emphasizes our heart and words in order to deemphasize works as the means to a right relationship with God. We don't enter into this covenant of salvation through Jewish law and tradition, or even through descent from Abraham. We enter into it by declaring Abraham's kind of faith, now centered on God's redemptive plan through Jesus.

The next three verses emphasize the universality of the gospel. It's for anyone. In 10:11, Paul finishes a quote he began in 9:33—those who believe in this cornerstone will not be shaken or ashamed (Isaiah 28:16). This applies to Greeks and Jews, as Israel's God is also the Lord of all creation (Romans 10:12). He responds to *everyone* who calls to him (10:13; Joel 2:32; Acts 2:21). Just as there is no difference between Gentiles and Jews in their sinfulness (Romans 3:22), there is no difference between them in their righteousness in Christ. God generously gives his grace to all who believe.

Paul suggests that a remnant will be saved (9:27; 11:5), but it's important to recognize that this is a rather pivotal remnant that begins with Israel, will extend to the ends of the earth, and ends with uncountable multitudes around God's throne (Revelation 7:9-10). Israel's rejection of its Messiah and God's mission to the Gentiles are not plan B in the redemption story. They were God's idea from the beginning.

RE-ENVISION THE INVITATION

Believing in your heart and confessing with your mouth is not just a ticket to heaven. It's an emphatic statement that you believe salvation is thoroughly initiated and achieved by God rather than human beings. It's a life of internal rest rather than internal struggle, a relationship rather than a religion. You've been given two options: getting right with God by applying yourself or receiving a right relationship with him by opening your heart and mouth. By choosing the latter, you are fully buying into God's plan—and fully able to live out the peace, freedom, and victory he has given you.

How can they hear about him unless someone tells them? And how will anyone go and tell them without being sent? That is why the Scriptures say, "How beautiful are the feet of messengers who bring good news!"

10:14-15

God has a way into everyone's heart, and he tailors it to their uniqueness. Still, there's a common progression: faith from hearing messengers who are sent. The messengers, their words, and the means by which they are sent may vary, but reception of the Good News always comes down to some version of this sequence. It's a foundational passage for preachers and missionaries everywhere.

"Who has believed our message?" (10:16) is a quote from Isaiah 53:1, the beginning of a passage that prophesies the rejection of the Messiah by his own people—a profoundly relevant chapter for this discussion in Romans. Paul follows this quote with more Old Testament references that demonstrate how his perspective is not a novel idea. Why would Israel's rejection of its Messiah be surprising, based on its history of rejecting prophets? God repeatedly warned them and disciplined them, even while maintaining his covenant and giving them hope. That's exactly what is happening here, Paul says. The covenant hasn't failed. God's chosen people have hardened their hearts, and his discipline may be painful, yet he has not rejected them and will not abandon them.

This is why a continued effort to send and preach so people will hear is important, among both Jews and Gentiles. It's how the Kingdom advances. The gospel is "Good News" because it keeps the door to salvation open, even for those who have initially refused to enter it. As long as people are hearing the message from messengers who have been sent, that door remains open.

RE-ENVISION THE GOOD NEWS

Throughout chapters 9–11, Paul is looking at a long history of people resisting God's ways because they thought they already knew them. They even resisted good news because it wasn't *their* news. It didn't fit the categories they had created or fulfill the demands they assumed God had placed on them. It was too easy. One of their assumptions seems to have been that if a message is too good to be true, it probably is.

But even though this particular message seems too good to be true, it's from God. It doesn't just free us from oppressive religion; it draws us into an exhilarating, enlivening relationship. Many Christians have rightly rejected "easy believism"—a casual assent to Christian beliefs—but wrongly continued to see God as a hard master. Reject that image. Trust and expect God's continuing generosity in every area of your life. From beginning to end, your relationship with him is based on good news.

A REDEMPTION PANORAMA

Has God rejected his people? By no means! . . . At the present time there is a remnant, chosen by grace.

11:1, 5, ESV

Paul has made the case that Israel as a nation (though certainly not all its people) had a long history of apostasy—the prophets give ample evidence of that. Some Gentiles, including those in Rome, may have wondered whether the Jews' rejection of Jesus meant God was now permanently rejecting them. Paul's answer to that in 11:1-12 is emphatic: "By no means!" In fact, Israel's continuing role in God's plan is a major theme of this letter. God could never turn his back on his own promises. Even a remnant of believing Jews proves that God's plan for Israel isn't aborted. And Paul himself is among that remnant, as are Jewish believers in Rome. Just as in Elijah's day (11:2-5), Jewish believers were not as alone as they might have thought. God would preserve them, even while using the hardened hearts of their compatriots to open the hearts of Gentiles.

Paul addresses Gentiles specifically in 11:13-24, reminding them that Jewish rejection of the gospel helped fuel the Gentile mission, resulting in the salvation of many of his readers. Gentile fruit comes from a Jewish root, which will make the root all the more glorious when Jews eventually do accept the gospel (11:15). Though Israel is more often pictured as a vine or vineyard (Deuteronomy 28; Isaiah 5), it is also pictured as an olive tree—in the context of judgment in Jeremiah 11:16 and of restoration in Hosea 14:6, a fitting illustration of how

Israel is both judged and restored by God. Paul adds another element in between: the grafting of new, non-native branches (Romans 11:17). His stern warnings against Gentile pride (11:18-20) point to tensions in the Roman church—typical Roman contempt for Jews may have spilled over into the church—but branches have no reason to feel superior to one another. They can be broken off at any time, and branches from the original tree can be grafted back in. God places all of his people in the same tree.

In fact, this regrafting of Israel will happen once the "full number of Gentiles" enters into the Kingdom (11:25-27). Jews will one day turn en masse to their salvation by grace through faith. Those who oppose this gospel (for now) play an important part in the redemption story (11:28). God still loves them and their ancestors and honors his promises to them. He doesn't revoke his gifts and calling (11:29). Every group of people has lived through seasons of rebellion so God could have mercy on all (11:32).

This chapter presents a sweeping picture of redemptive history and prophesies dramatic influxes of people into God's Kingdom. It also recognizes some hard truths. If Jews had widely accepted Jesus immediately, the church would have continued as a Jewish movement, and Gentiles might never have felt welcomed into it. Because most Jews rejected Jesus in the first century, Gentile believers became the abundant fruit of their Jewish root. And neither can claim superiority over the other.

RE-ENVISION SPIRITUAL MOVEMENTS

Like Paul, learn to view history through the lens of God's brilliant, unfathomable purposes. Read between the lines of geopolitics to see how his truth is changing hearts and his Kingdom is advancing. Reject the negative spin of surveys, critics, and cynics. More people believe in Jesus now than in any other time in history, and more are coming to him daily. However much or little our generation sees of God's overarching plan, he is accomplishing all his purposes and filling the earth with his glory.

SET APART FOR GOD

Since Abraham and the other patriarchs were holy, their descendants will also be holy—just as the entire batch of dough is holy because the portion given as an offering is holy. For if the roots of the tree are holy, the branches will be, too.

11:16

Paul assumes that Abraham, the patriarchal family, and Israel were all *holy*. If we equate holiness with righteousness, we might question his claim (and that of many biblical passages), but holiness and righteousness are not the same thing. Though many people throughout Israel's history were (by human standards) righteous, faithful, and godly, many others were not, as repeated prophetic warnings and an eventual exile demonstrate. Yet God called them holy anyway.

Holiness means being consecrated for a specific purpose, set apart or reserved for special use. We associate it with being pure because the God who consecrates us for his purposes is pure; but (hypothetically) a morally neutral god could set us apart for his purposes without requiring any purity at all, and that calling would fit some definitions of holiness. We need not concern ourselves with such distinctions; God is righteous, pure, and holy, and he makes his people righteous, pure, and holy too. But we do need to recognize the biblical emphasis on what we are made holy *for*—that is, an intimate relationship with God and the specific purposes he had in mind when he created us.

Paul still considered Jews to be holy, even as many rejected Jesus. They had lost sight of where they fit in God's plan, but they were still a very significant part of it. And because the root of the tree was holy, so were the branches. The call to be holy (1 Peter 1:16, quoting Leviticus 11:44) and our identity as a holy people (1 Peter 2:9; Colossians 3:12) run throughout the New Testament as they did through the Old. We have been grafted into a tree that God has long cultivated for an extraordinary, exceptional calling.

RE-ENVISION YOUR HOLINESS

You are holy. As a believer in Jesus, that's your identity and calling, whether you realize it or not—just as Paul addressed many of his readers as holy even when they were not acting very holy at all (1 Corinthians 1:2, for example). In Jesus, you are set apart for a unique, wholehearted, exclusive relationship with God. He has planned great things for you.

That's part of what it means to be a living sacrifice (Romans 12:1). It doesn't mean you should fill your life with "thou shalt nots," but God may call you to refrain from some things that other Christians do freely, or undertake some things that other Christians don't do, because of the purpose or assignment he has given you. But when you realize the enormity of your calling, those lifestyle adjustments aren't burdensome. Your *yes* to God makes every *no* to something else worthwhile. Your holiness is purpose driven, never works driven, and always treasured by the one who calls you to himself.

FRUITFUL BRANCHES

You Gentiles, who were branches from a wild olive tree, have been grafted in. So now you also receive the blessing God has promised Abraham and his children, sharing in the rich nourishment from the root of God's special olive tree.

11:17

Bible scholars have long debated the relationship of Jews and Gentiles within God's redemptive plan. And though the details are not systematically laid out in Scripture, Paul presents a revealing illustration here. God has planted a tree of salvation in this world, and it is rooted in the patriarchal family he chose when he called Abraham into a covenant with him. Abraham's descendants—in the flesh by many accounts, but through faith as Paul has argued from Scripture—are branches of that tree. God can break his branches in judgment (Jeremiah 11:16), and he can make them flourish (Hosea 14:6). And as Paul insists in Romans, some branches grafted into that tree are Gentiles, descendants of Abraham not by birth but by faith.

Clearly this image does not portray a replacement of Israel by the church. It describes one people of God who, through their faith in his redemptive purposes, remain connected to the root of Abraham and the God who called him. Gentiles are grafted into this tree not in order to keep Jewish law but to experience Jewish chosenness through Jesus and bear the fruit of his Kingdom.

By faith in Jesus, we can receive all the blessings God promised Abraham and his children.

Those blessings are many, and they include being made into a great people, passing on a great inheritance, and seeing others blessed through us. The idea of being "blessed to be a blessing" may come across as a simplistic cliché, but it contains a profound truth. God lavishes his goodness not only *on* us but also *through* us.

RE-ENVISION THE BLESSING

If you see yourself as a recipient of the blessings given to Abraham, you will be nourished by that root and can anticipate the fruit of generational promises. Abrahamic blessings don't trickle down to you; they flow right through you. You are among the many families of earth that have been blessed by that covenant, and others can be drawn into those blessings through you. Picture yourself as a conduit, a vessel of God's goodness. Envision yourself overflowing with God's favor for the sake of those around you—even if you don't feel full right now. God doesn't simply save you; he fills your life with saving graces that others can experience too. Pray for that, expect it, and live as an heir of age-old promises that change the world.

THE FAITH OF GENERATIONS

Notice how God is both kind and severe. He is severe toward those who disobeyed, but kind to you if you continue to trust in his kindness. But if you stop trusting, you also will be cut off.

11:22

God did not spare some branches (11:21)—a frightening concept that for many Christians raises the question of whether we can lose our salvation. Some biblical passages seem to suggest that we can, while others (even in this letter) imply that we cannot. It's a pressing issue for some, but not for those who believe God, love him, and continue in their faith however imperfectly. Such branches are never cast away.

Paul has already discussed God's kindness (2:4) and his wrath (1:18; 2:5-9; 5:9; 9:22). Here he emphasizes our responsibility to remain in his kindness rather than in unbelief—that is, to continue to believe in the gospel of salvation by grace through faith instead of turning away from it. After all, if God severed the branches of unbelieving Israel, who were once part of the tree, he could sever unbelieving Gentiles too—which serves as a warning against any sense of Gentile superiority toward Jewish believers (11:18-20). Apparently pride and judgment were problems in the Roman church (see also 2:1-3, 17-18, 23; 3:9, 27; 12:3, 16), but God's impartial kindness and severity undo pride.

Our cultural lenses may cause us to read Scripture individualistically, but that's not Paul's emphasis here. He has been talking about the collective rise and fall of believing and unbelieving generations (certainly with individual exceptions among them, Paul included). His focus has been on majorities, specifically why most of Israel has not followed their Messiah while many Gentiles have. But entire generations of Gentiles, like the Jews before them, could also find themselves at odds with God. The question of eternal security aside, Paul addresses the responses of people groups as a whole.

RE-ENVISION HISTORY

God chose to reveal himself through one family, who would have many descendants who would bless the world (Genesis 12:1-3). Why? Because revelation requires a context of individual and corporate experience. Israel served as that context for centuries, but salvation and a relationship with God were never just for one people group. All humanity had fallen, and all humanity needs the opportunity for restoration. The vessels of revelation found it difficult to embrace that new vision.

Practice seeing yourself as a vessel of revelation, a human context for divine activity and truth. This is your calling. Your life is a platform for demonstrations of God's presence, power, and purpose. Whether you think you are qualified for this calling, or are currently experiencing it, is not the point. Learn to think this way and the fruit will come. Amid social trends, culture wars, and even clashes of civilizations, you are a testimony of God's kindness. Live that role fully as a branch firmly supported by his enduring faithfulness.

IRREVOCABLE

God's gifts and his call can never be withdrawn.

11:29

God never revoked the gifts and calling he gave to Israel, regardless of how the Jews responded to their Messiah. That was important information for any Gentiles in the Roman church who might have thought God was done with his once-chosen people. But in God's faithfulness to an unfaithful Israel, we see a much bigger truth. God is faithful to all his gifts, callings, and promises. It's his nature to keep his word.

Most Romans had contempt for Jews—that eastern race that had unpatriotically secured an exemption from participating in the emperor cult, which included sacrifices to (or on behalf of) Caesar and a declaration that Caesar was lord. "God-fearers" in Roman society—Gentiles who believed in the Jewish God without going through the steps toward conversion—would have defended Jews and honored Israel for its place in God's plans. But even for those who believed in Jesus, associating with Jews may have felt a little uncomfortable. And some may have wondered whether Israel's place in God's plans still held true.

According to Paul, it did—perhaps not as the Jews expected, but as God had always planned. God still loves Jews because he chose their forefathers (11:28). He still honors the gifts he gave them as bearers of his covenant, laws, and glory (9:4-5). And because it's God's nature to keep his word, his faithfulness to Israel applies to all. He doesn't regret giving gifts or take them back once they are given. Whatever he has promised will be fulfilled.

RE-ENVISION YOUR CALLING

If you've ever felt like you missed your calling, Paul's assurances should be profoundly encouraging. You may have missed out on some of the specifics of your assignment, but you still have the gifts God has given you, the heart he filled with his desires, and the purpose he designed you to fulfill. He doesn't regret giving you any of that, and he isn't going to take it back from you. He will still empower you to do what he is calling you to do, and he still assures you with his promise that he will finish whatever he started in you (Philippians 1:6). Rest in that assurance. Never look at your past as a lost opportunity. God is faithful by nature and a restorer at heart (Isaiah 61:7; Joel 2:25; Zechariah 9:12). Recapture your vision, see yourself in alignment with the calling he has given you, and trust that his favor and blessing will follow you.

THE DEPTH OF HIS WAYS

Oh, how great are God's riches and wisdom and knowledge! How impossible it is for us to understand his decisions and his ways!

11:33

No one has figured out the unfathomable depths of God's purposes. That's why we consider them unfathomable. Sometimes we get glimpses of how brilliant and beautiful they are, and we marvel at his wisdom; and sometimes we're simply confused by things that don't make sense. We don't have to worry about understanding everything he does. In fact, we should be glad we don't. An infinite God grasped by finite minds would hardly be worthy of worship. And God is certainly worthy of ours.

That's why Paul ends his discussion of Israel's place in God's redemptive purposes with a doxology. His words have explained a lot, but even he acknowledges that God is doing something greater than we can describe. Though this amazing turn of events—how Israel's temporary transition to backstage actors opens center stage for Gentile believers for a time—had been in Scripture all along, it was only discernible in retrospect. God's salvation is much bigger than his people had imagined, and his glory will be even greater because of it.

God is much more interested in our faith than our understanding, which relieves us from the pressure of grasping the depths of eternal wisdom while also turning our focus to our own part in his plan. We don't have to figure out what he is doing through everyone else. We do have to respond to the calling he has given us. And part of that calling is to worship him for the riches and depths of his wisdom.

RE-ENVISION MYSTERY

The Christian faith has been under attack since the time of Jesus and declared dead or dying in quite a few generations. We've been told that churches are losing members at alarming rates, missionaries are achieving paltry results, and secular culture has triumphed over our backward views. Yet nearly a third of the world's population identifies itself as Christian, at least nominally,* and movements around the world are reaching generations and people groups once thought to be unreachable. Those with eyes of faith can see revival breaking out and expect more to come. There are signs of another Great Awakening, this one greater than any that have come before. Despite the mixed—or even dismal—messages we've been given, God is doing amazing things.

How? That's a mystery that unfolds over the course of time, and we get to see only a moment of it during our time on earth. But we can trust God with whatever we cannot see, and know that, in time, every knee will bow and acknowledge that Jesus is Lord. That promise is always a cause for praise.

* "Share of Global Population Affiliated with Major Religious Groups in 2022, by Religion," Statista, accessed July 18, 2024, https://www.statista.com/statistics/374704/share-of-global-population-by-religion.

ROMANS 12:1–15:13

LIVING IN THE BIG PICTURE

After his panoramic view of God's sovereign purposes—and how both Jewish and Gentile believers may have misunderstood them—Paul turns now to our appropriate response: *offering ourselves to God in worship*. We become living sacrifices who live and think differently from the way the world thinks and from the ways we've thought before (12:1-2). Specifically, we learn to see ourselves and others accurately as members of one body characterized by love and honor (12:3-13), and we learn to see the non-believing world, even our adversaries, through the lens of love and mercy (12:14-21). We relate to government not as the enemy but as authority derived from God (13:1-7). And we take a whole new approach to living rightly, not driven by external demands but by internal love (13:11-14).

Chapter 14 addresses a practical matter that was causing some division in the Roman churches. Believers held different opinions on what was appropriate to eat and drink, as well as which days were to be observed as holy. These were not unusual disputes in the early church or anywhere Jewish and Gentile Christians gathered, especially as fellowship and hospitality created numerous occasions to eat together. Gentile and Jewish dietary practices differed widely—they were among the key distinctions between Israel and surrounding peoples for centuries—and now believers from different backgrounds were having to negotiate a common understanding. Friction was inevitable, and Paul tries to help them sort it out, always bringing them back to the big picture of love, grace, and the character of God's Kingdom.

BACKGROUND

Gentile readers of Paul's letters may have been both fascinated and a little uncomfortable with his (and of course Jesus') emphasis on love. Most Romans highly valued pride, status, and receiving honor. Love for anyone other than empire, family, and one's closest friends was often considered a character flaw, a sign of weakness and vulnerability. The idea of sacrificially loving acquaintances, strangers, and enemies was a stretch. Yet this is the hallmark of the body of Christ, the common bond of the new humanity, and new believers knew this sacrificial love was the foundation of their relationship with God and others—even if it came with a bit of discomfort.

The Christian movement developed during the Pax Romana, the "Roman Peace"—a roughly two-hundred-year period from the time of Augustus to the late AD 100s. Roads facilitated travel, the Roman military enforced the peace (though often violently), Caesars claimed lordship and salvation as "sons of god" (and expected subjects to honor them as such), and the empire generally flourished, at least in general political and economic terms, if not for everyone.

Persecution against Christians broke out at times—not across the empire or for great lengths of time, but in certain locations and long enough for victims to wonder when it would end. One of those persecutions was under Nero's rule, just a few years after Paul wrote to the Romans. We might wonder whether Paul's instructions in 13:1-7 would have changed if he had known of Nero's abuses at the time of writing, but the principles he bases his teaching on are timeless enough. Authority derives from God (even when it isn't godly), and Christians should not undermine earthly governments, though our ultimate loyalty is to a higher King. We stand to benefit in a society of order, and we gain greater influence when promoting it. Greater influence serves our mission as agents of renewal and restoration in this world.

Paul turns to matters of eating and drinking in chapter 14. One of the reasons God gave Israel its law was so they would be distinct from the idolatrous peoples around them. Their faith was to be a testimony for all, but God wanted them to remain cultural separatists, to a degree. This new era of Gentile inclusion among God's people raised some volatile issues, particularly the Gentiles' relationship to Israel's laws and traditions, and especially their need to distance themselves from sexual immorality and idolatry (see Acts 15:1-21).

Peter's first visit to a Gentile home had stretched him well beyond his comfort zone, but God made it clear that he was to go (Acts 10–11). Hospitality norms in the ancient world (and many cultures today) dictated eating whatever was offered, which meant Peter would have to dine with Cornelius and his household. The backlash he received for partaking of nonkosher food was at first intense; and even after it was clear that the Holy Spirit accepted Gentiles apart from the law, many Jewish believers continued to insist that Gentiles follow the law as Christians (see Galatians 2:11-14). This was a source of ongoing tension throughout much of the first century.

Dietary questions seem to have been one of the practical issues causing disagreement between Jewish and Gentile believers in Rome—not whether it was okay to eat any nonkosher food, necessarily, but whether one should eat meat without knowing how it was prepared or whether it had been used in idolatrous sacrifices. Paul addresses this issue (along with the observance of certain days) in Romans 14 (and also 1 Corinthians 8), focusing primarily on bridging divides rather than supporting one side or the other.

THE BIG PICTURE

Paul offers many details in these chapters, but the overarching issue is what our new life in Christ should look like. Up to this point, the letter has laid strong historical-theological foundations for the new humanity God planned long ago and has now birthed through Jesus' life, death, and resurrection. But such strong foundations always have practical implications for our thoughts, words, actions, and relationships. These chapters spell out much of that.

As should be obvious by now, this is not just about living up to a standard. It's about embodying the nature and character of God, which is thoroughly centered on love. And because we have been made right in our new life, it's about demonstrating the reality of the new creation and making the world right again. We aren't just saved *from* a fallen, sinful, futile existence. We are saved *into* a new creation and *for* spreading that newness around us. And it will always be energized and characterized by love, honor, peace, joy, and rightness in the Spirit of God.

THE PUREST WORSHIP

Dear brothers and sisters, I plead with you to give your bodies to God because of all he has done for you. Let them be a living and holy sacrifice—the kind he will find acceptable. This is truly the way to worship him.

12:1

In a letter appealing to Gentile and Jewish believers to see themselves on level ground and as equal members of the people of God, Paul addresses his "brothers and sisters" in Rome. He is making a case for unity, positioning his instructions in this chapter (and elsewhere) as a family matter. And they follow naturally from what he has just said—that God has dealt with Jews and Gentiles in a way that extends mercy to as many as possible and most fruitfully grows the tree of his Kingdom. He has just praised God for his unfathomable wisdom and knowledge. This plea to present our bodies to God as a living, holy sacrifice is the logical outcome of all he has written to this point.

This reasonable, sensible, acceptable worship is therefore a natural response to what God has done. If we really understood the majesty and beauty of his plan, we would gladly give ourselves to him. We would trust him implicitly with our entire selves. Instead of bringing sacrifices to the altar according to the law of Moses, we should bring ourselves to the altar according to the law of the Spirit that sets us free. But unlike those old sacrifices, we don't die. The sacrifice of ourselves keeps us alive and set apart for God's exclusive use.

Paul laid the groundwork for this sacrifice earlier. Our old humanity has been crucified and buried with Christ so we can be resurrected with him into new life (6:3-5). God sent his Son in our kind of body and gave him as a sacrifice for us (8:3). Now in 12:1 (as in 6:13), we take on his Spirit and live as a sacrifice for him. We leave our old life behind and receive his new life forever as an all-encompassing act of worship.

RE-ENVISION SACRIFICE

Many of us have come to faith with a prayer something like this: "*Lord, everything I am and everything I have belongs to you. I'm yours.*" Over time, our inward attitude may imperceptibly shift toward another perspective: "*Lord, I need you in my life. Please work this out for me . . .*"

There's nothing wrong with petitioning God for something, but we need to see ourselves as his treasured possession. As Paul writes in 1 Corinthians 6:20, we've been "bought . . . with a high price." God isn't just a part of our lives. He *is* our life, and our lives are his.

See yourself as fully given over to God's purposes. Go all in. It's hardly a sacrifice to receive all that he is in exchange for all that you once were. The more you lay down your life, the more he fills your life with his own. You have nothing to lose by losing everything for his sake. You gain everything in him.

A NEW MIND

Don't copy the behavior and customs of this world, but let God transform you into a new person by changing the way you think. Then you will learn to know God's will for you, which is good and pleasing and perfect.

12:2

Giving ourselves wholly to God as living sacrifices involves a radical change of culture. Like a foreigner in a new land, we transition from the old humanity to the new, from the dictates of the world to the environment of the Kingdom. We can't do that without a transformation, which includes being born of the Spirit, learning to walk in the Spirit's power (8:1-16), and living in the freedom we've been given.

That transformation also includes aligning our thoughts with what is already true about us. This entire letter has been aimed at radically reorienting our thinking—see especially 6:1-14 and 8:1-14—because the gospel requires an entirely new worldview. The Greek concept of repentance emphasizes changing the way we think, a nice complement to the Hebrew concept of repentance, which emphasizes a change in behavior. Full repentance involves changed thinking that results in a changed life. By allowing our minds to be renewed, we discern God's will and live new lives.

In fact, genuine, lasting behavioral change always begins with a new way to think, which is why Paul has emphasized images of burial and resurrection (6:1-4) and how to "consider [ourselves] . . . dead to the power of sin and alive to God" (6:11). When we *see* differently, we *live* differently. Our old selves were accustomed to distorted ways of seeing God, ourselves, other people, and our circumstances, leading us into confusion and misguided decisions. Paul is essentially telling us here to change our vision, to live with a new narrative in our minds. We need to see God for who he is, see ourselves for who we are, see other believers for who they are, see the world for what it is, and more. When our vision is clear, we can know God's good, perfect, and pleasing will.

Transformation is an ongoing process, as the verb tense suggests. But more and more, we are learning to see everything with new eyes through the lenses of the Kingdom. As living sacrifices, we receive truth, allow it to change us, and experience the new creation.

RE-ENVISION RENEWAL

In your transformation process, listen to the soundtrack in your mind. If it's worried about what might or "probably will" happen; if it's rehearsing conversations you've had or might have with contentious people; if it's anticipating failure or lack; if it's lamenting past mistakes or what life could have been; if it's bitter toward those who have done you wrong; if it's filled with disgust for everything on the news and all the wrongheaded opinions people have; if it's eating you up with insecurity or shame; it is out of sync with the Spirit—these are not God's thoughts.

What if the soundtrack in your mind wasn't filled primarily with to-do lists, relational concerns, potential problems, and all the other things you tend to think about, but instead with worship and gratitude? It would change your attitude and perspective, which would change what you do and say, which would fundamentally alter the course of your life.

Dwell on God's goodness. Trust his love and kindness. Believe what he says about you. Fully embrace every promise he gives you. Accept your adoption and inheritance as a member of the family. Rehearse truth constantly and declare it out loud. Over time, your vision and thoughts will be transformed, and your life will be too.

MUTUAL BELONGING

We are many parts of one body, and we all belong to each other.

12:5

What does a renewed mind think? For one thing, it gives us an appropriate perspective of ourselves (12:3). We are unfathomably valuable, but so is everyone else in God's Kingdom. God wants us to think of ourselves as beloved children in whom he delights, but we need to see other believers that way too. Paul has made it clear that we can no longer measure ourselves by how well we've done—that is, by our works. If we're going to measure anything about ourselves, it needs to be our faith.

Most of all, we are to see ourselves as members of one body. In the old humanity, our natural instinct may have been to build ourselves up and tear others down. That's a zero-sum game that turns the world into winners and losers. In the new humanity, life in the body is a positive-sum game, a win-win situation. We build ourselves up by building up the body. We value everybody's part in the whole.

There's a reason Paul emphasizes an appropriate self-perception as members of a larger body. He is likely addressing divisions between Jewish and Gentile believers. Based on his efforts to level the ground in the first three chapters and his frequent comments about pride and boasting, each group seems to have been looking down on the other. Early in the letter, he brought them all low.

Here (as in 5:1-2) he raises them all to extraordinary heights. The humble are being exalted, just as God said. But they need to be exalted without losing their humility.

RE-ENVISION YOURSELF

It's human nature to see ourselves in relation to other people, but comparison usually leads to one of two results: either looking down on other believers or looking up to them. Give honor where honor is due, but refuse to live with a mental measuring stick. When you compare yourself to others, you will likely become either proud or insecure, neither of which is an accurate self-perception. Paul calls you to re-envision yourself as incredibly loved and valued, but just as incredibly loved and valued as other people. You are one treasured member of an immeasurably treasured family, a sharer of all God's blessings, which are plentiful enough to go around—and, in fact, increase as we spread them widely. Let yourself—and others—experience them as fully as possible.

PARTS OF THE WHOLE

In his grace, God has given us different gifts for doing certain things well.

12:6

When Paul wrote to the Corinthians about spiritual gifts (1 Corinthians 12), he addressed their unhealthy competition to vie for the most prestigious ones and show how gifted they were. Here he seems to address gifts in the context of church members minimizing their need for each other—specifically Jews thinking they already had a long track record with God and didn't need what newcomer Gentiles had to offer, and Gentiles thinking the Jewish experience with God was irrelevant if the law of Moses didn't apply to them. But Gentiles needed to know the redemption story and where they fit in it, which they couldn't do without valuing Jewish believers. And Jewish believers needed to understand the new work God was doing, which they couldn't do without valuing the Gentile experience.

That meant appreciating the range of gifts God had given. It would make no sense for a Gentile to appreciate another Gentile's prophetic voice while dismissing that of a Jewish believer (or vice versa), or for a Jewish believer to value the leadership of other Jews but undermine the leadership of Gentiles (or vice versa). And believers of any background who might have been reluctant to assert themselves in the congregation needed encouragement to do so. If God has given one person a gift, it's to be used for the benefit of everyone.

That's always the case. Every gift God has given his people is for the good of all. No one gets them all, of course; God insists that we benefit from each other. We don't lose our individuality, but we do belong to each other as members of the same body. God has designed us to be interdependent and calls us to live complementary lives.

RE-ENVISION THE BODY

Some Christians see their relationship with God as a purely private matter, but Scripture portrays life in the body of Christ as a shared experience. Faith may be very personal, but you can't experience God as fully as he wants without the gifts he has given other people, and they can't experience him as fully as he wants except through your gifts. The full relationship necessarily involves other believers.

Some people are more relational than others, but even the most reserved among us have a vital place in the fellowship. You are spiritually connected to other believers. Their growth depends on you, and yours depends on them. See the body as a whole and yourself as an irreplaceable member, and freely offer other members all the gifts God has given you.

THE BODY OF CHRIST AS MANY

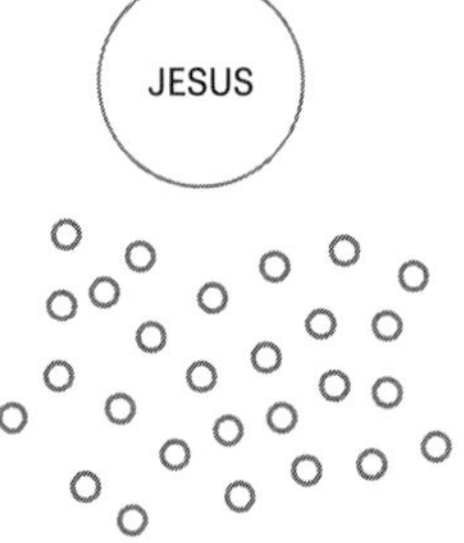

THE BODY OF CHRIST AS ONE

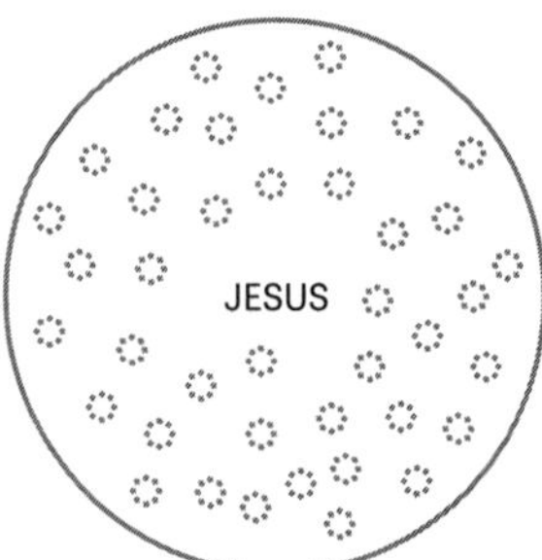

Envisioning the whole: When we see ourselves and other believers as distinct entities with disparate interests, motives, and purposes, we tend to individualize and compete. When we see each other as members of the same body, we're much more likely to look out for the welfare of others. Their well-being is connected to ours, and the body can flourish as one.

AFFECTION AND DELIGHT

Love each other with genuine affection, and take delight in honoring each other.

12:10

In Roman culture, love was often considered a weakness. Self-interest was entirely understandable, and pursuing your own honor at the expense of others was expected and considered shrewd. There were exceptions—sacrifice on behalf of Rome or one's own family was honorable—but empire and family could fall into the category of self-interest. In the minds of most Romans, sacrifice for neighbors and strangers, especially those of a lower status, didn't make sense.

Human values in a fallen world are distortions of truth. Love and sacrifice are among the highest values in God's Kingdom. Love is the priority—central to God's nature—and it is to be expressed to everyone, including those of lower status and even our enemies (12:15-21). For living sacrifices whose minds are being transformed, these heavenly values should present no problem. We came into the Kingdom through God's extravagant love for the unworthy. Loving others extravagantly should become natural.

Paul's instruction to love each other with genuine affection literally conveys the idea of outdoing each other in giving honor or being exceedingly eager to honor others. It's a subtle dig at Romans who would compete for highest honors for themselves; believers should subvert that rivalry by giving honor rather than seeking it. That kind of competition isn't divisive. It unites the fellowship in mutual esteem.

Love has many implications, some of which Paul spells out in 12:11-13. Living sacrifices with renewed minds are zealous for the well-being of fellow believers. The culture of the new humanity rearranges our values and prioritizes the fellowship of faith. We end up looking radically different from the world around us.

RE-ENVISION LOVE

At its heart, our cultural reorientation in the new humanity is based on making a very significant shift. Idealists in the old humanity advocate for this shift but rarely realize it, but those who have received new life from Jesus and are empowered by his Spirit can. As our minds are renewed, we move from a self-focused life to an other-focused life. No longer do we reach for better and more, always taking in. We add to what God has poured into us by also pouring it out, knowing that whatever we pour out will be multiplied and given back to us (Luke 6:38). In short, we love others as we have been loved.

See yourself not as a sail needing to catch the wind of others in order to thrive but as the wind that fills their sails. This is how the Spirit of God—the wind of his nature—empowers his people. He breathes love into each one of us and then sets us free to breathe love into our fellow believers. Fully forgiven and accepted, we have nothing to earn, no need to compete, no insecurity to compensate for, no honor to strive for. We are free to simply live, love, give, and honor until everyone's sail is full.

BLESSERS BY NATURE

Bless those who persecute you. Don't curse them; pray that God will bless them. Be happy with those who are happy, and weep with those who weep. Live in harmony with each other.

12:14-16

Just as many Romans viewed love and sacrifice as pointless, many would have found it absurd to show kindness to an enemy. Roman politicians and military leaders—overlapping categories, in many cases—often advocated harsh treatment of adversaries. But in the new humanity, adversaries are candidates for God's grace and ours as well. The only way to bring people into a Kingdom of love is with love.

Paul has been describing our relationship with other believers, the body of Christ. Even believers with competitive instincts can understand the purpose of love within the fellowship. But how should we relate to people outside of the body? Even if those people have positioned themselves as our enemies, God wants them to be blessed. Paul, once an enemy of Jesus and his people, would know this better than most. God blessed him with a radically new life and purpose. The mercy of an undeserved blessing is powerful.

How can we bless those who persecute us? It isn't possible unless we know deep down that we are radically forgiven and free—and that this forgiveness and freedom can change any life and is available to all. Just as someone overflowing with gratitude for having been blessed with enormous wealth finds it easy to be generous, someone overflowing with gratitude for having been loved, healed, and set free finds it easy to be loving and offer healing and freedom to others. When we really understand what we've been given, we want others to have it too.

RE-ENVISION ENEMIES

We have a connection with other believers, and that connection makes it relatively easy to treat them sympathetically. We don't have that connection with nonbelievers—unless we begin to envision them as potential members of the body of Christ. They are not enemies; they are wounded souls facing all kinds of battles that result in distorted views, misplaced values, and unreasonable hostility. They don't need pushback; they need a touch from God. And by virtue of your connection to them, you're the one to give it to them.

Decide to be unoffendable. Become a blesser by nature. Just as God blessed you based on *his* goodness and not yours, bless others according to what they need, not what they may deserve. The best way to love your enemy is first to know how much you yourself are loved (1 John 4:19). Immerse yourself completely in that love. Let it sink in. Then allow it to overflow to everyone around you—across all lines of division, and even to your adversaries.

THE POWER OF GOOD

Don't let evil conquer you, but conquer evil by doing good.

12:21

If the culture and lifestyle of Romans 12 sounds familiar, it should. Much of it comes from the teachings of Jesus, particularly in the Sermon on the Mount. There we are told to turn the other cheek, go the extra mile, bless those who persecute us, love our enemies, take care of those in need, and be peacemakers. Paul has touched on all these same instructions, positioning them in the new life we've been given. Living sacrifices with new minds see the world in radically new ways.

Not only does this chapter clearly reflect Jesus' teachings; it also reflects his actions. He lived sacrificially, expressed love to all and honor where it was due, valued every person appropriately, blessed his enemies, and overcame evil with good. He was so thoroughly secure in his identity that he did not need to compare himself to others, compete for honor, or vindicate himself in the face of accusations or threats. He loved freely because it was his nature.

With no need to compensate or compete, we are free to "live in peace with everyone" (12:18). Peace may not be possible in every relationship, and we aren't told to force the issue. But we can always do our part to reconcile, while leaving room for God to work in any situation (12:19). Whatever "burning coals" means in 12:20 (a quote of Proverbs 25:21-22), Paul's point is to be generous with our enemies. Doing good may intensify that person's awareness of his or her offense, possibly provoking a change of heart. In any case, regardless of appearances, good overcomes evil. No adversary has the upper hand on us when we demonstrate divine mercy. The God of restoration will be honored by our efforts to bring peace into a contentious world.

RE-ENVISION PEACEMAKING

Jesus is our model, and the only way to conform to his character and nature is through the Spirit-empowered lifestyle presented in Romans 8 and the sacrificial, thought-transforming, other-centered lifestyle described in Romans 12. No one can live out these instructions to love and honor everyone without first knowing how deeply they themselves are loved, accepted, secure, fulfilled, and set free. In short, the gospel makes us mentally strong and emotionally healthy. What we have freely received, we are able to freely give.

That's the heart of peacemaking in this world. It isn't just about resolving conflict. It's about experiencing the fullness of life in Christ and blessing others with its fruit. Like moths drawn to a flame, the wandering, fluttering denizens of a fallen, futile world are often drawn to the light of God's people—*if* his people know who they are in him and are living out of the fullness of his character. Be one of those people, and let God burn brightly in you.

GIVING HONOR WHERE IT'S DUE

Everyone must submit to governing authorities. For all authority comes from God, and those in positions of authority have been placed there by God.

13:1

Throughout Christian history, Paul's instructions on relating to authority have raised as many questions as they've answered. But it's important to remember the context: the expulsion of Jews (or at least prominent Jews) from Rome in AD 49 that ended with the death of Claudius in 54. In the absence of Jewish leaders, Gentiles had taken leadership of the Roman church, and when Jewish believers returned, many may have harbored resentment and mistrust of the Roman government for what they had been through.

Few Romans made much of a distinction between Jews and Christians, so attitudes toward one might easily have been applied to the other. And Roman leaders could be heavy-handed toward factions they disliked. Paul understood the need for believers to be model citizens. Just as they were learning to see God, themselves, other believers, nonbelievers, and adversaries differently, they also needed to see the government differently. Paul's words in this chapter show them how.

The idea that all authority comes from God was something of an affront to Caesar (in this case, Nero), who would have seen his authority as divine and himself as something resembling a god. This letter was written before Nero had clearly demonstrated his hostility toward Christians, but the principle of submitting to authorities remains even afterward. Political authorities may not be godly, but their function is God-given. They keep peace and order—an important role that follows logically from what Paul has just written about enemies and vengeance. This is not an exhaustive statement on our responsibility toward governments, as some laws (such as those compelling Christians to confess, "Caesar is Lord") clearly should not be obeyed. In confessing Jesus as Lord, Christians had already confessed that Caesar was not. As Peter and John demonstrated when they continued to preach in Jerusalem but were willing to suffer the legal consequences for doing so (Acts 4:19-20), there's a balance between our faithfulness to God and our obligations to government.

Of course, Paul is not defending corrupt or abusive governments. He's simply saying that wherever governments don't directly contradict God's purposes and ways, we should honor their policies and decrees. Honor is highly valued in God's Kingdom, and if we're going to honor the invisible God, we need to understand how authority works and honor our visible rulers. We don't have to agree with them, but we should support them to the extent we can without violating our commitment to God.

RE-ENVISION AUTHORITY

Even though there is enmity between the systems of this world and the Kingdom of God, avoid seeing them as direct opposites. Yes, you ultimately serve God's Kingdom over earthly kingdoms, but these are overlapping spheres, not completely separate ones. Your willingness to submit to earthly authorities strongly reflects your willingness to submit to God. Recognize which authority is higher and eternal, but honor both however you can, trusting God to give you peace and influence in the world.

THE LAW OF LOVE

Owe nothing to anyone—except for your obligation to love one another. If you love your neighbor, you will fulfill the requirements of God's law.

13:8

Paul has written a lot about the law in this letter. Nowhere has he told us that the law is wrong or that we shouldn't keep it, only that keeping it won't put us in a right relationship with God. Still, we need to know how to live, and the unifying theme of God's law shows us how to do that. At the heart of all God's commandments is an overarching purpose: *love*.

Love was the subject of much of chapter 12, and Paul returns to it in chapter 13 after explaining our relationship to governmental authority. Love is a much higher law than the Mosaic covenant and any empire's decrees. Jesus declared that all the demands of God's laws and his prophets are based on the commandments to love God and love others. John noted twice that God *is* love (1 John 4:8, 16), and Paul wrote of the primacy of love in one of Scripture's most eloquent and memorable chapters (1 Corinthians 13). God's core attribute is the driving force behind creation, our relationship with him, and our relationships with the people around us. Love is God's nature and is at the heart of everything he does.

Laws tell us what to do without empowering us to do it. They can tell us to love others, but they cannot turn us into loving people. Love inspires us, motivates us, and fills our thoughts, words, and actions with power. It also makes laws unnecessary. If we love our neighbors, we don't need to be told how to treat them. Someone full of love will behave lovingly, fulfilling the heart of the law without consciously obeying it. When we have genuine love, we look a lot like our Father.

RE-ENVISION RELATIONSHIPS

As living sacrifices, we often approach God with the question, "Lord, what do you want me to do?" It's not a bad question, but it isn't the first one we should ask. An even more important line of questioning is this: "Lord, what spirit is driving me? What are the motives behind my thoughts, words, and actions?" The answer to aim for, of course, is the Holy Spirit. If God is love, so is his Spirit. Our questions about what to do will often be answered by the Spirit, who moves us even before we ask.

See yourself as a vessel of love with the power to transform the atmosphere around you. The environment shifts and lives change—including your own—when you love well. Seek no other motive, and live according to the Spirit at work within you. There is no greater law to fulfill than the law of love.

A NEW DAWN

The night is almost gone; the day of salvation will soon be here. So remove your dark deeds like dirty clothes, and put on the shining armor of right living. . . . Clothe yourself with the presence of the Lord Jesus Christ. And don't let yourself think about ways to indulge your evil desires.

13:12, 14

Paul's vision of our new life—the transformation from old humanity to new—is as dramatic as night and day. In fact, he uses that exact image on more than one occasion (see also Ephesians 5:8-14; 1 Thessalonians 5:4-8), as well as the idea of taking off the old and putting on the new as if we were dressing in an entirely new wardrobe (Galatians 3:27; Ephesians 4:22-24; Colossians 3:8-14). These two images are paired in Romans 13:11-14, with our old humanity fading away into the darkness and the new coming in brilliance and beauty. After all, says Paul, the hour is late.

In fact, Paul speaks of salvation as future (13:11-12), even though we are already saved. We have been born of the Spirit, our sinful nature has been put to death, and our salvation is already complete. Even so, the vestiges of sin—old thought patterns and habits, for example—linger on, which is why we have to renew our thinking (12:2), and our bodies have not yet been resurrected (8:23-25). Though we have received our salvation in full, we haven't yet experienced it in full, much like a baby is fully human but hasn't yet experienced the fullness of that humanity. But the complete experience of our salvation is getting closer.

We can experience it more abundantly by living in the light and putting on our new wardrobe. We no longer need to live from base impulses that were ingrained in us as fallen human beings. We are no longer compelled by humanistic reasoning that suggests we are driven purely by brain chemistry, hormonal urges, and survival instincts. We've been given higher motives and an eternal perspective that shape everything we think, say, and do. Our worldview is lit up with the glory of eternity. Why return to the shadows of ignorance, confusion, and despair? New creations see everything in new ways, and that vision drives our lives.

RE-ENVISION YOUR CULTURE

You are a new creation, a member of the new humanity. That transition to new life is an even bigger adjustment than moving to a new country and trying to assimilate to its culture. In renewing your mind, you are learning to dress like a Kingdom citizen, changing your customs, adopting new ways of speaking, and becoming sensitive to the cultural cues that mark you as an insider. You are putting on Jesus as if you were dressing in an entirely new suit of clothes.

This new life as a child and heir of God is more than "right living." Putting on the "armor of light" (13:12, ESV, NIV, NKJV, NASB) involves a clear perspective, rays of love and joy within your heart, a rightness of heart, pure motives, spiritual power and purpose, and letting Jesus fully live his life within you. Like Romans called to leave behind a pagan lifestyle or Jewish believers leaving behind old assumptions about the law and righteousness, shed every vestige of the shroud of darkness and clothe yourself in the light of God's glory and grace.

ON MATTERS OF CONSCIENCE

Accept other believers who are weak in faith, and don't argue with them about what they think is right or wrong.

14:1

Much of the meat sold in Roman and Greek cities came from animals that had been sacrificed to idols. This made Torah-observant Jews wary of any markets that would not verify the source of their meat and whether it had been drained and prepared properly—in other words, whether it was clean or unclean. But these standards did not translate easily into Gentile Christianity, and debates abounded—particularly in the case of food associated with idolatry. Jewish believers generally kept kosher, and some ate only vegetables to avoid any violation of their beliefs (14:2). Many Gentiles considered these concerns (and the observance of certain days) to be minor issues, as long as their intentions were good. Who was right? According to Paul, this was a matter of conscience and no cause for finger-pointing.

In Galatians, Paul comes down hard on *Judaizers*—Jewish believers who insisted that Gentiles should keep the law God had given. He seems to address the opposite problem in Romans—the insistence of Gentiles that Jewish believers leave behind centuries of ingrained (and God-given) beliefs about food and drink. Those who ate meat indiscriminately apparently looked down on those who didn't. And those who kept kosher seemed to have little patience for those who lacked such discernment. At least one side (and perhaps both) considered the other side *weak*.

This contempt for those who are seemingly less spiritual is not an exclusively ancient phenomenon. It continues in our day. But it doesn't strengthen the fellowship, reflect God's grace, or give appropriate emphasis to faith. It assumes a right to judge "someone else's servants" (14:4), much like a stranger inappropriately rebuking other people's children. God knows how to correct his children when they are ready for it, without relying on criticism and squabbles between them.

RE-ENVISION DOS AND DON'TS

Paul's discussion centers on food, drink, and sacred days, but the larger issue is what a community of grace looks like. The New Testament clearly shows us that cultural differences should present no threat to Christian unity; but because we often have difficulty distinguishing between absolutes and matters of conscience, those differences may divide us. Paul has spent the last two chapters describing the culture of God's Kingdom, and it has little to do with eating, drinking, and observing certain days (14:17). The focus is instead on love, honor, grace, and mutual support.

In all your relationships with other believers, choose grace. Recognize God's desire to train and correct each of his children in their own seasons and stages, just as he has done with you. See yourself as a champion and cheerleader for all who have placed their faith in Jesus, and give them—and yourself—room to grow.

HIS TRUSTWORTHY LEADING

So why do you condemn another believer? Why do you look down on another believer? Remember, we will all stand before the judgment seat of God.

14:10

Our tendency to look down on some people is natural—according to our old nature. But as Paul has made clear, we've been given a *new* nature, and it changes the way we see others. Rather than our instinctual judgments—even if they're based on our Bible-based convictions—we default to grace. God has liberally given us grace, and we in turn share it liberally with the people around us.

Our approach to matters of conscience should be guided by two principles. We should be "fully convinced" in our own hearts (14:5), and we should be motivated by gratitude and a desire to honor God (14:6). If we are being led by the Spirit (8:5-11), we ought to *trust* the Spirit to actually lead us. And if we trust him to lead us, we can trust him to lead other people too. Our focus is not on whether they are following him well. It's instead on God's ability to parent his own children according to their own personalities, needs, and seasons of growth.

Whatever mutual accountability God has called us to offer one another, it doesn't include judgment. God will take care of that himself. Every believer will stand before him, not to receive a verdict on their salvation—that has been secured by our new birth, our resurrection in Jesus—but for rewards and recompense in his Kingdom (1 Corinthians 3:10–4:5; 2 Corinthians 5:10). We will give our own account to him (Romans 14:12), and much of it will concern the extent to which we supported and encouraged our fellow believers.

RE-ENVISION GRACE

We live at a time in history when everybody assumes the right to comment on other people's lives—and social media makes it easy. We've created a toxic culture that intensifies our feelings of guilt, shame, insecurity, defensiveness, and reciprocal judgment. It looks nothing like the culture of the new humanity.

Like every human being, you will one day stand before God's judgment seat. He won't ask you about other people's decisions, only yours. The welfare of the entire body of Christ is certainly our mutual concern, but we can be grateful that its diversity is not ours to manage. It's too immense and complex for any of us.

Even so, our experiences, testimonies, wisdom, advice, and encouragement are essential for the fellowship of believers. Resist the "oughts" and "shoulds" and judgments that can so easily fill our thinking, but share your perspectives freely. As you do, respect the perspectives of others as well. See every follower of Jesus as a case study in how God grants both conscience and freedom to his people, and marvel at his ways. Our gate into the new humanity is as narrow as a single Savior, but the fields of his grace, mercy, and guidance are vast enough for all of us. Celebrate God's wisdom in leading us to them.

FREEDOM AND FAITHFULNESS

Each of us will give a personal account to God. So let's stop condemning each other. Decide instead to live in such a way that you will not cause another believer to stumble and fall.

14:12-13

God told Peter to go to the home of Cornelius, a Roman centurion. Peter had never entered a Gentile home or eaten nonkosher food (Acts 10:14, 28), so this visit would take him far beyond his comfort zone. But having followed Jesus for three years, Peter was used to uncomfortable situations. So he went, explained the message of salvation to a group of Gentiles, and watched in amazement as the Holy Spirit fell on all of them. Then he received an unsurprising backlash from fellow Jewish believers who were appalled at his association with non-Jews (Acts 11:1-3).

Paul rejected that kind of condemnation often and emphatically, as he does in chapter 14. But the people who criticized Peter—or in the context of Romans, the people criticizing each other for choices about food, drink, and sacred observances—could use Paul's words for their purposes too. Exactly who was causing whom to stumble? If, by accepting Cornelius's hospitality, Peter offended Jews, was he not a hindrance to potential Torah-observant believers? Can't freedoms and prohibitions cause equal amounts of stumbling?

Paul almost always erred on the side of freedom and made concessions only when they were expedient for fruitful ministry (as in Acts 16:2-3). He often offended the self-righteous but was bothered by offenses that hindered the growth of new or immature believers. Recognizing that flaunting our freedom can be disorienting to some, he urged caution and mutual support.

Even so, his instructions here have been widely misinterpreted. It's impossible to prevent all offenses. Real righteousness is neither lawless nor legalistic. We don't want to cause anyone to stumble, but we can't be held responsible for every person's reaction or misunderstanding. A fear of "hints" of sin that aren't really sin has created a culture of Pharisaism in much of the church. It's good to be faithful in the details of daily behavior, but even better to be faithful in the major issues above those details.

Jesus is our example. He nurtured faith but did not cater to religious expectations. Otherwise he never would have dined with tax collectors, talked with the Samaritan woman at the well, healed on the Sabbath, let a prostitute touch him with her tears and her hair, or put himself in a position to be called a glutton and a drunkard. He presented a picture of true righteousness, even if the self-righteous were offended.

RE-ENVISION DEVOTION

Many Christians are far more diligent about peripheral issues than about demonstrating a heart of love, compassion, justice, peace, joy, truth, and grace. Many tend to focus more on their politics than on their calling to real transformation—as if changing laws ever changed anyone's heart. As Jesus put it, they "tithe herbs" at the expense of bigger issues (Matthew 23:23). Both are important, the latter immensely more so.

Never codify the guidance God has given you. View other people not in terms of what the Holy Spirit is doing in you but what he is doing in them. Partner with the Spirit in his ministry to all who are growing in faith by helping them grasp the new humanity's true freedoms and responsibilities. Resist other people's legalism, but live out your freedom wisely.

THE KINGDOM CULTURE

The Kingdom of God is not a matter of what we eat or drink, but of living a life of goodness and peace and joy in the Holy Spirit.

14:17

It has been an epic battle in many periods of church history. On one side are those who live out their freedom in ways that other believers may not be able to understand or accept. On the other side are critics of cheap grace and casual spirituality that don't account for God's holiness. Each charges the other with turning people away from the faith and disrupting the fellowship. Yet somewhere between law and liberty is a greater truth and a higher calling—the heart of the Kingdom of God.

Paul was very familiar with these battles and often found himself right in the middle of them. His letter to the Galatians was birthed in this context, and much of his ministry among the Gentiles was opposed by Jews on these grounds. He vehemently opposed Jewish believers who insisted that the full experience of Israel's salvation included full acceptance of Israel's legal covenant, even if its laws were only an expression of righteousness rather than the means to it. He saw all such wrangling as a distraction from the big picture.

The big picture is the nature of the Kingdom. It isn't about eating, drinking, observances, prohibitions, permissions, and other peripheral matters. These all have a place—as matters of individual conscience—but living in the Kingdom is not about rituals and regulations. It's about radical transformation. We've been called to live lives of true righteousness, goodness, peace, and joy in the Holy Spirit. Religious practices related to earthly elements are minor details.

RE-ENVISION KINGDOM LIFE

Watch what the Holy Spirit is doing across the body of Christ. If you look closely enough, you'll see him at work in people who hold very different views on the Christian life. If he doesn't treat those issues as deal-breakers, neither should we. If he isn't keeping his distance from those who embrace a certain practice or insist on a certain freedom, we have no reason to keep our distance either. We certainly have no cause to break fellowship over such things.

The real question is how well we see the big picture and whether we have chosen a behavior-driven life or a Spirit-driven life. Both have behavioral implications, but only one honors the desires, motives, and persona of the Spirit within us. Any approach to the Christian life that comes down to "just tell me what to do" falls far short of God's desires for us. He wants us to be sensitive to his voice, his movements, and his motivations in the moment—which may not be the same every moment. He is not a formulaic God, and he will not be codified. He will only be known relationally in an environment of goodness, peace, and joy.

HIS EYES AND OURS

Blessed are those who don't feel guilty for doing something they have decided is right.

14:22

Behind the chaos of Israel's era of judges—the period between its entrance into the Promised Land and its first kings—is a sobering indictment: "All the people did whatever seemed right in their own eyes" (Judges 21:25). For people who had been given a detailed law and divine covenant and told that their well-being depended entirely on their faithfulness (Deuteronomy 28), this was a problem. They were not called to do what was right *in their own eyes*. They were called to do what God had already told them was right.

Here Paul urges Christians to rely on their conscience to deal with gray areas in the life of faith. It would be a terrible piece of advice for people not born from and filled with God's Spirit, but in light of our intimate relationship with God, the Spirit's empowerment within, and the promise of abounding grace, it's liberating. Unlike the people in the book of Judges, we aren't doing what is right in our own eyes out of rebellion or ignorance. We're doing it from a desire to be faithful.

This conscience-based approach to practical living doesn't apply to everything, of course. Some moral issues are quite clear. But for those that aren't, the intention behind our behavior is decisive. If we think something might offend God and do it anyway, we've sinned (14:23). If we're confident something will not offend God, even if others believe it will, we are free to follow our convictions if it doesn't cause others to stumble. Paul wrote to another congregation that "'all things are lawful,' but not all things are helpful" (1 Corinthians 10:23, ESV). But there's another gauge beyond *helpful*: aligning our attitudes and attributes with the Spirit.

RE-ENVISION YOUR CONSCIENCE

Most people see their conscience as a subjective guide. Perhaps it is, but for believers in Jesus, our conscience is guided by the Holy Spirit. If you let him, he will use your inner compass to steer you in his ways.

Do you have confidence in the Spirit within you? Many people place much greater faith in the power of sin to trip them up than in the power of the Spirit to keep them standing. If fear of sin is stronger within you than confidence in the Spirit's guidance, that's a sign of two things: a distorted vision and a tendency toward principles rather than relationship. God's grace is greater than all our sin, and he fills us with his wisdom, power, and love. He trusts the Spirit he has put within you. You can too.

COLLEGIAL CHRISTIANITY

We should help others do what is right and build them up in the Lord.

15:2

Most Christians see the body of Christ as a collection of individuals. We may gather on Sundays and other times for fellowship, but we live out our faith independently. Many Christians also see their particular branch of Christianity as the fullest expression of faith and others as deviations from it. Modern society has distanced us from a deep sense of oneness in Jesus.

God's Kingdom is more than a collection of individuals. It's a united, organic whole. Much of Paul's teaching in the last few chapters is based on that sense of unity—a collegial, symbiotic Christianity in which every person's welfare is our own. Their suffering is ours (and ours theirs); their faith struggles and ours are connected; and members of the body mutually support, encourage, and strengthen each other. We are bound by something much stronger than family genes. We are all filled with the same Spirit working out his purposes for us, in us, and through us together.

Paul emphasizes honoring and supporting each other regardless of our diverse perspectives on the details of living out our faith. It isn't enough for us to do the right thing and build ourselves up. We are to build up others as well and help them do the right thing—not by telling them what to do but by encouraging their faithfulness.

This mutual blessing extends well beyond interpersonal relationships. The body of Christ benefits when congregations focus outward. When churches pray for other churches—even those with different practices and perspectives—the body of Christ is strengthened. So is our testimony to our culture.

RE-ENVISION SYMBIOSIS

Avoid competitive Christianity. Many Christians have bought into the toxic culture of complaint, but it doesn't reflect the culture of God's Kingdom. Disagreements over relatively minor issues of doctrine or methodology have turned into charges of heresy, with plenty of finger-pointing and strident defenses of "why we're different." Christian denominations and movements have, in many cases, turned exclusive rather than mutually supportive.

Envision a Christian culture in which people from different doctrinal or methodological backgrounds pray for each other, meet for fellowship, build bridges, and honor each other's place in the Kingdom. It's a beautiful picture, isn't it? Now having envisioned it, go out and live it—and encourage others to do the same. People with a new nature are comfortable with new connections and eager to build up others in the Lord.

THE LONG STORY OF FAITH

Such things were written in the Scriptures long ago to teach us. And the Scriptures give us hope and encouragement as we wait patiently for God's promises to be fulfilled.

15:4

For Paul, "the Scriptures" were what we know today as the Old Testament, and he quoted from them liberally in Romans and his other letters. This was not to advocate for reliance on Israel's law—much of Romans has distanced salvation from that law—but he does urge us to fully accept Old Testament promises and let them stir up our faith and hope as we wait for their fulfillment. In fact, we can't really understand the New Testament apart from the Old. In Scripture as a whole, we see the purposes and heart of God and are encouraged to know him deeply.

It's possible to read Scripture and miss the point, of course. Scribes and Pharisees knew the words but missed the heart behind them. Unfortunately, Christians have a long history of doing the same thing—using the Bible to reinforce injustices, neglecting foundational truths and principles, and even resisting innovations such as Sunday school and missions organizations because they were "unbiblical." But Spirit-led people find hope and encouragement in those words. More importantly, we see the nature and character of God.

In 15:3, Paul uses a messianic prophecy (Psalm 69:9) to show how Jesus was more concerned about other people's interests than his own rights and privileges—a model for us in all our relationships with other believers. That's what should guide the debate about religious and cultural practices. Are we asserting our rights or looking out for our fellow Christians? Either way, our internal stance will dictate our external behavior. One approach builds up the body; the other tears it apart.

All of Scripture is useful for building up the body (1 Corinthians 10:11; 2 Timothy 3:16-17)—not only for knowing what to do, but also for seeing who we were created to be and how we are redeemed, re-created, restored, and empowered. Through it, we see our place in God's plan and fulfillment. It brings us life.

RE-ENVISION SCRIPTURE

As you read the Bible, envision yourself as part of the long narrative of God's people, a member of the spiritual family of Abraham by faith (Romans 2:29; 4:9-25), an insider rather than an outsider (regardless of how other people see you), a brother or sister of Jesus, and an heir of the promises (8:15-17). When you read Scripture, you are not just a reader of the redemptive story; you're a character in it. You occupy the same stage, only in a later act. In fact, as much as you may look up to the heroes of faith, they were looking ahead to you (Hebrews 11:39-40). Follow their example and be encouraged, knowing that they would marvel at the faith you have received.

VOICES OF ETERNAL FELLOWSHIP

Accept each other just as Christ has accepted you so that God will be given glory.

15:7

Paul urges "complete harmony" among "followers of Christ Jesus" (15:5). He has in mind the tensions between Jewish and Gentile believers in the Roman church, of course—his words in 15:8-12 address each group's role in redemptive history, with several Old Testament prophecies of Gentile inclusion—but his point is well taken across cultures and ages. Like beautifully blended voices sounding as one, God's people are to sing his praises and give him glory for eternity, including now.

Accepting each other as Christ has accepted us is the central truth and summary of Paul's discussion that began in 14:1 (even stretching back to 12:3-5). Spiritual, emotional, and material hospitality is an essential attribute of God's people. God has shown it to us and extends it to others through us. As Jesus told the Twelve, "Give as freely as you have received!" (Matthew 10:8).

Throughout this passage, and really all of Romans, Paul has envisioned an uncontentious, unpretentious, unoffendable fellowship, with each member living in deference to one another, each more eager to see what the Spirit is doing in the other than to assert what he is doing in oneself. A truly Christian culture is ideally selfless and other-centered—what many utopian dreamers have imagined as their own invention. The voices in this community will likely never sing in unison, but we can certainly sing in harmony, bringing to God a compatible diversity of personalities and experiences and a unity of spirit that pleases him and reflects his love. This was his plan from the beginning—a global body of Christ representing numerous nations, peoples, languages, testimonies, and perspectives. Many members make for one enormously coherent whole.

RE-ENVISION HARMONY

It is painfully clear that vestiges of sinful habits and attitudes remain even in the new humanity, and no Christian community has fully developed an ideal culture. But we still aim for it. It's our calling, and one day we will experience it completely. The testimony of Scripture assures us.

Make this your vision too. You will see plenty of contradictions to it, but don't be discouraged by them. Keep moving in the direction of harmony, drawing others into it. The more we see ourselves as inextricable parts of the whole—irreplaceable voices that contribute to the eternal harmony—the more we will bring heaven's environment to earth. And the more God will be glorified in our time.

THE SOURCE OF HOPE

I pray that God, the source of hope, will fill you completely with joy and peace because you trust in him. Then you will overflow with confident hope through the power of the Holy Spirit.

15:13

Paul wrote earlier that Abraham believed God even against all hope (4:18), that endurance and character produce the kind of hope that does not disappoint (5:5), that we hope in what we do not yet see (8:24-25), that Scripture gives us hope as we wait for promises to be fulfilled (15:4), and that the God of hope will fill us with overflowing hope if we believe. We might get the impression that Roman Christians were discouraged and faltering in faith. Whatever the reason for that—external pressures, internal tension, or something else—hope is always warranted in God's Kingdom. When we live in hope, our lives make a profound statement about God's goodness. We are in sync with him.

Many Christians are living without any hope other than their expectation of heaven one day. While that hope is paramount and very real, it is not the sum of our hope in God. The journey of faith should be filled with anticipation and wonder, even when we go through trying times. Jesus acknowledged that we would experience tribulation in this world, but his declaration that he has overcome the world glistens like an open invitation engraved with gold (John 16:33). Paul has built upon that invitation by urging us to see ourselves as overcomers in Christ (Romans 8:37). If Jesus overcame the world and we are in him, we are never truly defeated.

Paul's call to hope in today's verse bases it on the joy and peace that come from faith and the power of the Holy Spirit, who fills us with it. Many believers miss out on this joy, peace, and hope because they don't really believe what God says about them. They are trying to *become* somebody, be righteous, recapture the divine image, and reach for something more, even as God says they *are* somebody (his beloved children), are righteous *now*, have *already* been given the divine image, and are *heirs of all things* in Christ. What's left to strive for? It's all ours by faith.

RE-ENVISION YOUR EXPECTATIONS

Choose to live a life of overflowing hope, recognizing that this is in fact a choice. You may need to train yourself in it—many people do, and it can take time—but tell yourself the truth daily. Reorient your focus. It's human nature to fixate on whatever is wrong and needs to be fixed, but the new humanity focuses on what's right and the fulfillment that is coming. Biblical hope is not wishful thinking but waiting for what is certain, and there's nothing speculative about it. You are simply looking ahead to what God has promised.

As you renew your mind with hope, also re-envision your life as the stage on which God demonstrates his goodness. Learn to expect his generosity in every area of your life, whether you see it right now or not. Know that his blessings and fulfillment are comprehensive. When peace, joy, and hope rise up within you like a fountain of living water, let them overflow. This is the life God has promised you.

ROMANS 15:14–16:27

PEACE, HOPE, AND A WORLDWIDE VISION

Paul has made his case—many of them, actually—and cast an enormous vision for what God has done throughout history, is doing in the new Jesus movement, and will do in restoring the world through his people bearing his image and glory. He ends his letter with some formalities common to most ancient letters. But as with anything Paul writes, these formalities come with explicit and implicit appeals, encouragements, and exhortations.

As many ancient letter writers did, Paul states his credentials (15:15-20), not to boast but to lend weight to his words. Echoing the beginning of the letter (1:10-15), he expresses a desire to visit these Roman believers, sharing with them his planned itinerary, and casts a vision for future ministry (15:23-29). He urges them to participate in this ministry by praying for him (15:30-32), knowing that his upcoming trip to Jerusalem poses threats. He (along with Phoebe as the deliverer of the letter, Tertius as the actual writer of it, and Timothy as Paul's co-worker) sends greetings to many of his readers by name, having numerous connections among Roman believers through various past experiences. It's an eclectic list—men, women, Latins, Greeks, Jews, elites, commoners—that tells us quite a lot about the Roman church and the households that hosted their meetings. Paul's formalities, as usual, are enlightening.

Though this section of the letter is not filled with teaching, it nevertheless adds to our vision of God's purposes. Paul's sense of mission, his hopes for going to distant places such as Spain, and his close and extensive ties with other believers of all backgrounds leave us with the impression that the new humanity—the renewed and restored bearers of God's glorious image, no matter how few in number they are at the time of this letter—represent the fulfillment of God's purposes from the beginning of time.

BACKGROUND

Paul often made it clear that he was a Jew called to spread the message of redemption to Gentiles, as God had told Ananias at the time of Paul's encounter with Jesus (Acts 9:15), and in fulfillment of ancient prophecies that God would eventually extend his Kingdom and salvation to Gentiles. The plans he shared with the Romans reflect the extent of that calling. He had been ministering in Macedonia and Achaia, both culturally Greek; he had been as far as Illyricum (modern Albania, Serbia, Bosnia, Croatia); he would soon return to the Jewish homeland; and he hoped to go as far as Spain, the western end of the empire.

All these places were Roman provinces, but they were very different in geography, climate, social norms and structures, religion, and other cultural dynamics. Linguistically, they were united by Latin and Greek, though Paul would have found far fewer Greek speakers in Spain than in any place he had ever been. Depending on how much Latin he knew, he may have expected some linguistic challenges there, including a need for interpreters to reach many in his audience. Clearly, he firmly believed the gospel could cross cultural and linguistic boundaries and was meant for the whole world.

Paul's desire to visit Rome is not at all surprising. His first missionary journey covered much of Asia Minor. His calling to Macedonia (Acts 16) during his second journey took him to Europe (though no ancient would have seen the world in terms of our modern division of continents). God was obviously sending him to the far reaches of the known world, at least in a westward direction (other early Christians took the gospel to other places). Politically, Rome stood at the center of the world (as Paul conceived it), as the hub of the empire. Rome's Caesar was widely acknowledged as lord. Where better to proclaim the true Lord than at the seat of earthly power? Where better to preach the eternal Kingdom than in the place dubbed by Latin poets as "the Eternal City"?

The number of Christians in Rome was probably not huge, but neither was it insignificant. They had influence and a reputation (Romans 1:8; 16:19), and Nero could not have made a statement by persecuting them, as he did a few years after this letter was written, if they weren't prominent and numerous enough to matter. The fact that the church remained strong after this persecution suggests they had become a significant minority in the city. And as Paul's greetings attest, they spanned social, economic, ethnic, and gender divides.

THE BIG PICTURE

Paul has presented the gospel as the inauguration of a new humanity. His agenda and network reflect the breadth and depth of this new creation. His outlook also implies a calling for every believer. As Paul has made clear throughout this letter, the gospel is not just about how God renews and restores us. It's about what he does *through* us—how he is renewing and restoring the world through his people. This can only happen if Israel is God's *firstborn* nation, not his only born nation. All who believe are grafted into God's people, and all become catalysts for transforming the world. Paul's expansive vision has huge implications. It can't be fulfilled unless believers see first what God has done for them, and then what he is doing through them.

This is why, in Romans, Paul has not simply presented the Good News of salvation as it is often understood. He has presented the Good News of the *Kingdom*, a theme emphasized in all four Gospels and throughout the New Testament. Nowhere does Romans tell us that we are escaping this world. In fact, just the opposite. As Paul's missionary vision and the fellowship of Roman churches demonstrate, we are at the center of the new earth, both as evidence and as agents of renewal.

FULLY PRESENTING THE GOOD NEWS

They were convinced by the power of miraculous signs and wonders and by the power of God's Spirit. In this way, I have fully presented the Good News of Christ from Jerusalem all the way to Illyricum.

15:19

Writers in ancient times often emphasized their credentials for their readers. This rhetorical practice bordered on boasting, and Paul was typically hesitant to indulge himself (15:18). Yet in writing to a church he had not helped establish and had never visited, his track record mattered. He wanted the Romans to recognize his authority without forcing it on them.

Paul's perception of his own credentials is revealing. His pedigree as a Pharisee (Acts 23:6; Philippians 3:5) was well known, and he has mentioned his Jewish heritage several times in this letter. But that isn't what he emphasizes in his brief résumé here. Above all, he wants to remind the Romans of his call to preach to Gentiles (Romans 15:16, 18)—as if to say, "I'm not just a member of the Jewish faction; I'm a bridge between the two groups in your church"—and how God's power has worked through him (15:17, 19). His message was not just in words. It was authenticated by changed lives and miraculous signs and wonders.

Paul connects the message with miracles elsewhere too, perhaps most directly in his first letter to the Corinthians, where he admits the weakness of his own presence and persuasion and relies instead on "a demonstration of the Spirit's power" (1 Corinthians 2:4, NIV). This is a pattern among all who preached the Good News in Acts, in keeping with the demonstrations of power in Jesus, who assured his followers that they would carry out the same kinds of works that he had (John 14:12). The point throughout the New Testament is that the gospel is more than just words and beliefs. It's the fullness of God's presence, purpose, and power. The Good News of Jesus centers on spiritual salvation from sin and death but also includes restoration from brokenness, futility, despair, regret, loss, and all the ravages of sin and a fallen world. The new humanity experiences an abundance of life.

RE-ENVISION THE GOSPEL

The gospel of salvation is the core of the Christian message, but it's not the full picture. Jesus presented the Good News of the Kingdom—not just information to respond to, not just a message to hear and accept, but a demonstration of the new humanity. This certainly includes information, preaching, powerful words, and the promise of eternal life, but it also involves hearts transformed by the Spirit, restoration of lives, reconciled relationships, and empowered ministry characterized by Jesus accomplishing his works in us and through us.

Even more than a gospel presentation, the world needs a gospel *demonstration*. The Good News of the Kingdom doesn't take us out of our fallen world yet, but it does bring healing, deliverance, and restoration to our lives—and through us, to the lives of others. Seek that fullness for yourself and for the world around you, always moving in the power of God and (like Paul) *fully* presenting the Good News of Jesus.

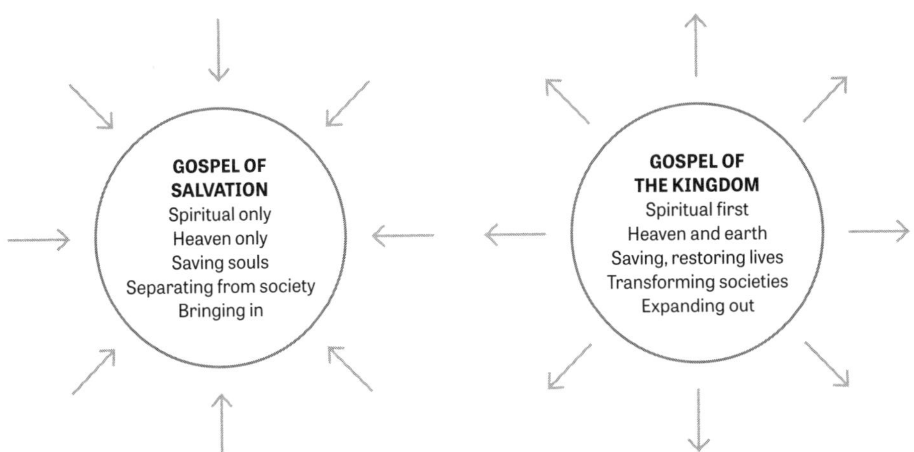

The gospel of salvation is part of the gospel of the Kingdom, but it's not the full picture. The gospel of salvation rightly demonstrates God's love for human beings and his desire for them to spend eternity with him. The gospel of the Kingdom does so, too, but also demonstrates God's goodness and the nature of his Kingdom in this world.

TO THE ENDS OF THE EARTH

The believers in Macedonia and Achaia have eagerly taken up an offering for the poor among the believers in Jerusalem. . . . Since the Gentiles received the spiritual blessings of the Good News from the believers in Jerusalem, they feel the least they can do in return is to help them financially.

15:26-27

Paul expresses his desire to visit Rome at both the beginning and end of his letter. Here he explains his past and anticipated itinerary. He has been busy preaching (and demonstrating) the Good News in places that have not yet been pioneered by someone else (15:20), and after a brief trip to Jerusalem (or so he expects), he hopes to go to Spain and drop in on the Romans on the way (15:23-29). One of his reasons for going to Jerusalem is to deliver an offering from churches in Macedonia and Achaia, the area from which he is writing this letter. Diaspora Jews regularly sent the Temple tax and offerings for the poor to support the homeland and the Temple in Jerusalem. Paul's efforts to continue this offering among churches effectively serves his purpose of maintaining ties between Jewish and Gentile believers. He is constantly deepening connections among Christians as the gospel goes global.

One of his purposes in mentioning his work among Gentiles, his trip to

Jerusalem, and the offering of the churches is to point out the connections that already exist between Jews and Gentiles elsewhere, even if they may be strained in Rome. These ties prove that Gentiles in other places honor Jews and the gospel's Jewish origins, and that Jewish believers have recognized and accepted God's work among the Gentiles. In other words, this relationship can work.

As we know from Acts, Paul will not make it to Rome the way he expects. He will be arrested in Jerusalem, imprisoned for two years as his trials slowly unfold, and eventually sent to Rome upon appealing his case to Caesar. Scholars debate whether he ever made it to Spain, but this peek into his itinerary and the desires and rationale behind it help us understand his sense of mission as well as the movements and expansion of the early church. As Jesus foretold (Acts 1:8), good news is truly headed toward the ends of the earth.

RE-ENVISION THE NETWORK

You are part of a global network. You see one piece of it up close at your local church, but it extends across political and geographic boundaries around the world. Many people enjoy calculating degrees of separation between various people, but the only degree of separation between you and any other believer in the world is geographic. In Christ, you are spiritually bound to one another. No matter how locally or regionally focused you are, your prayers, financial gifts, service, and relationships with other Christians enhance the body of Christ as a whole.

Live with that big vision of worldwide spiritual unity among the fellowship of believers. Pray daily for the church around the world. Bind your heart to all true Christians everywhere, near and far, even to the ends of the earth.

JOIN THE STRUGGLE

Dear brothers and sisters, I urge you in the name of our Lord Jesus Christ to join in my struggle by praying to God for me. Do this because of your love for me, given to you by the Holy Spirit.

15:30

Paul knew his trip to Jerusalem was risky. He was well aware of "those in Judea who refuse to obey God" (15:31)—the Jewish leaders most stridently opposed to the Jesus movement, as Paul himself once was. He understood the dynamics of his mission—the fierce opposition to the idea of Gentiles believing in a disgracefully crucified Jewish teacher without honoring Jewish laws and traditions; the precarious position of Jewish Christians in Jerusalem, who might be persecuted if Paul's presence intensified the conflict; and the volatile nature of religious reactions under the imperial eye. Vocal advocates of a controversial Messiah ran great risks in such a contentious climate.

As it turned out, Paul was right to suspect danger. He was arrested and spent more than two years in Judea awaiting trials, defending himself repeatedly before the Jewish council and Roman officials. Finally, after appealing his case to Caesar (his right as a Roman citizen), he was shipped to Rome, where he lived at least two years under house arrest, teaching all who came to him—likely including many of the recipients of this letter. His desire to visit Rome was certainly fulfilled, though not under the conditions he expected. He finally saw these Romans in person, "in the fullness of the blessing of Christ" (15:29, ESV), and that blessing included a surprising ministry to Roman soldiers and political elites.

RE-ENVISION THE MISSION

Millions of Christians around the world today experience similar dangers and threats, whether for teaching and demonstrating the gospel openly or simply for being Christians. Because we are all bound to each other in Christ, these are not the experiences of people "over there" somewhere. They are brothers and sisters, closer spiritually than any biological brother or sister. Every member of God's Kingdom is our spiritual kin.

We can't take on all the struggles of the Christian world, or even all of them in our own city or region. But we can each take on at least one. Choose an area of struggle, some desperate need, one intense front line in the advance of the Kingdom to adopt as your own. Join the struggle in prayer, as Paul asked the Romans to do, and add your voice and contributions in whatever ways you can. See it not as *their* problem, but as yours collectively. Solidarity is a Christian virtue. Envision every Christian mission as our mission together, and put your whole self into it.

A NEW FAMILY

Greet each other with a sacred kiss. All the churches of Christ send you their greetings.

16:16

Paul was writing from Corinth (or the nearby port city of Cenchrea), a Greek area with many Roman connections—a Roman colony that prided itself on its Roman-ness. Priscilla and Aquila had settled there temporarily after Claudius expelled the Jews from Rome. They are named in 16:3-5 as leaders of one of Rome's house churches, and many other people mentioned in this section of greetings had similar ties with Paul's ministry. Though he had not yet visited the place known to Roman poets as "the Eternal City," he knew many citizens of the truly eternal Kingdom who lived there.

Most of Paul's friends and co-workers in Rome have Latin or Greek names, even if they come from a Jewish background (like Andronicus and Junia, 16:7). More than a third are women, whom Paul commends for their ministry as freely as he commends the men. Phoebe, who delivers the letter from Cenchrea to Rome (16:1), is likely the first to have read it to the congregations and possibly fielded questions about Paul's meaning. Several house churches are mentioned or implied, suggesting diverse and numerous Christians in the city and the need for several copies of this letter to pass around.

Overall, throughout the letter and now in chapter 16, we get a sense that the Roman church collectively was growing, wrestling with important issues, and learning how to navigate the kinds of relationships created by their spiritual union in Christ. We can also assume they were dealing with external pressures from a Roman society that generally looked down on eastern religions like Judaism, monotheism in general, elites socially connected with servants and slaves (as happened often in the early church), devotees of any religion that bucked its civic responsibility (like the emperor cult), and certainly devotees of a leader who had been scandalously executed by Roman authorities. Unity was not only an ideal for Christian communities like this; it was often necessary for survival.

RE-ENVISION DIFFERENCES

Imagine marrying into a family from an unfamiliar, deeply traditional culture and trying as an outsider to learn its customs, perspectives, and beliefs. You and they might experience awkward moments and unintentional offenses as you adapt to each other, but because you're now members of the same family, you'll find a way to make it work.

This picture of blended families and cultures is similar to what first-century churches in Greek and Roman cities experienced. In Rome, as elsewhere, the relationship between Jewish and Gentile believers could be strained. So could the relationships between members of markedly different social strata, each gender, various religious backgrounds, and diverse political factions. In an appeal to unity, Paul wrote to the Galatians that "there is no longer Jew or Gentile, slave or free, male and female" (Galatians 3:28). This is an implicit message in the book of Romans too. They would all have to learn to love each other.

Embrace that vision for the church: diverse members of one body who have learned to love each other. Assume the best of everyone, gently deal with the worst when it comes out, and cultivate unity—without compromising truth, and always in Christ. This love is, as Jesus emphasized (John 13:35), the hallmark of the new humanity.

DEFENDING THE CORE MESSAGE

Now I make one more appeal, my dear brothers and sisters. Watch out for people who cause divisions and upset people's faith by teaching things contrary to what you have been taught. Stay away from them.

16:17

Paul has gone to great lengths in Romans to bridge divides and cultivate unity. It naturally follows, then, that his "one more appeal" to this spiritual family of his "dear brothers and sisters" would be against "people who cause divisions." Anything that contradicts the new humanity in Christ, anything that compromises our walk in the Spirit as living sacrifices with renewed minds, anything that weakens the bonds of love in this spiritual family should be firmly resisted.

This doesn't mean we should shun those who have somewhat different interpretations of Scripture or teach insights that are new to us. We need a diversity of perspectives in the body of Christ. It also doesn't mean we should try to keep the peace and preserve unity by not standing up for truth. Though we can't control the responses of those who break fellowship because they don't like what we believe, compromising our convictions for the sake of peace leads to a fragile, unhealthy peace. No, Paul is urging us to resist self-promoting agendas and distortions of the message of salvation by grace through faith. This is the gospel he is contending for throughout his letters.

The first-century Jesus movement was not monolithic. Major and minor doctrines regarding the meaning of salvation, the nature of Jesus, and the significance of his sacrifice were still being sorted out. So were the practical implications of this message. Paul was aware of and even comfortable with different perspectives. But not when those perspectives turned the gospel into something it's not.

RE-ENVISION TRUTH

Anchor yourself in the gospel of salvation by grace through faith and refuse to be moved from it. Envision that message as an unassailable fortress, with God as its guardian and every usurper attacking its walls as its nemesis. Learn to appreciate all the rich and insightful perspectives people share within that core message, but reject any sleight of hand that takes your attention off the resurrected life. Most of all, preserve the bonds of love and peace among those who believe without compromising the truth that created those bonds in the first place. As Paul said earlier (1:16), this gospel is nothing to be ashamed of. It is the power of God at work.

LIVING IN VICTORY

I want you to be wise in doing right and to stay innocent of any wrong. The God of peace will soon crush Satan under your feet. May the grace of our Lord Jesus be with you.

16:19-20

Genesis tells us that even before humanity sinned, God had a solution, and he began revealing it soon after the Fall. The serpent would strike the heel of the woman's offspring, but her offspring would bruise the serpent's head (Genesis 3:15). God's covenant with Abraham (Genesis 12:1-3) aligns with this prophecy, so we can include among "the woman's offspring" Abraham's descendants, the Hebrew people, and—more specifically—the nation of Israel. The heel that mortally bruised the serpent's head was that of Jesus, the suffering Messiah who turned the enemy's worst strike into his eternal defeat. Jesus won the decisive victory.

Jesus not only won that victory; he shares it with all who believe (Romans 8:37; Luke 10:17-19). Paul writes elsewhere that Jesus humiliated the enemy by stripping him of power and then gave the spoils of war to his people (Ephesians 4:7-8; Colossians 2:13-15). Jesus invites us to look to him for victory, but he also gives us the authority to win battles in his name. We overcome by his blood and our testimony (Revelation 12:11). God will do the crushing, Paul says, but we and the Romans share in the victory by believing, persisting in truth, and standing firm in the grace we've been given.

The victory Paul envisions here is over the false teachers who distort the message of salvation by grace through faith (Romans 16:17). Because the Roman believers knew the value of being "wise in doing right" and "innocent of any wrong," the enemy's strategies would fail. Even more, the enemy himself would be crushed. We are heirs not only of the promises given through Abraham and Israel. We're also heirs of the prophecy given in Eden.

RE-ENVISION THE STORYLINE

Imagine watching a movie when you already know the outcome: The good guys win, and the bad guy is put away for life. You may experience tension as you watch the story unfold, but there's no real suspense. You know how it will turn out.

Your life, and Christian history as a whole, involves a series of real-life "movies" that end with that kind of certainty. You haven't seen them before, but you can know that the enemy eventually gets defeated every time. He may seem to have power in various seasons of your life, but Jesus has given you authority over his power—with a promise that nothing will ultimately harm you (Luke 10:19). Every weapon of the enemy is temporary and essentially futile. Trust God when he tells you how this will end.

Refuse to see yourself under the thumb of the enemy—ever. You may experience brokenness, hardship, and pain, but you are not a victim. Once trapped in futility and decay, you are now resurrected with Jesus, a new creation, empowered by the Spirit, a living sacrifice pleasing to God, and an heir of all his promises—including the one about crushing the serpent's head. That's the vision Paul unfolds in Romans. Let it also be yours.

CONCLUSION

Paul ends this majestic letter with a blessing for the God "who is able to make you strong" (16:25). That in itself is a promise worth celebrating, especially for people who early in the letter were declared unrighteous and condemned, image-bearers who have fallen immeasurably short of the glory we were created to reflect. Much of Romans, even as it has addressed the friction between Jewish and Gentile believers and God's overarching plan for his people, has been aimed at restoring us to that glorious image. This image is included in our inheritance in the new humanity. Far from falling short of his glory now, we are beloved children and overwhelming victors in Jesus. Not only is God able to make us strong, but he already has.

Of course, we experience none of that strength, nor the fullness of our inheritance, apart from faith. We've been given salvation by grace through faith, but we experience its blessings as we open the eyes of faith to what God has said is true. So throughout the letter, Paul has given us images to envision and believe:

- ***Inheritance:*** Like Abraham, we are heirs of God's promises by faith and co-heirs with Jesus through our union with him (4:16; 8:17).

- ***A new humanity:*** Just as sin infected all through Adam, righteousness is given through Jesus to all who believe (5:12-21).
- ***Burial and resurrection:*** Our old selves are buried with Jesus, and we are resurrected with him in new life (6:1-14).
- ***Freed slaves:*** We once were slaves to sin, but being bound to Christ has set us free (6:15-23).
- ***The law as our widower:*** Like a surviving spouse, the law no longer has any claim on us. We have died with Jesus and been raised to a new kind of life (7:1-6).
- ***A groaning, longing creation:*** A world subjected to futility and decay longs to see redemption—in the children of God, our resurrection, and our future glory (8:18-30).
- ***Invincibility through love:*** Nothing in this world can separate us from God's love. We have overwhelming victory in him in all things (8:31-39).
- ***God the potter:*** The sovereign God oversees the rise and fall of peoples and their faith in him (9:14-29).
- ***The olive tree of faith:*** God's covenant is rooted in Abraham's calling and faith, but the branches of Jews and Gentiles can flourish, wither, be cut off, and be grafted in according to the seasons of redemptive history (11:16-24).
- ***The altar of sacrifice:*** Our greatest act of worship is to present ourselves as living sacrifices on God's altar. He is pleased to accept that offering and radically transform our lives as new creations (12:1-2).
- ***The body of Christ:*** The new humanity forms a new community that prioritizes love, lives responsibly, and supports each member selflessly (12:3–15:13).

These are powerful images. They are also invitations to immerse ourselves in these truths until they shape our identity and change our nature. The more we "consider ourselves" to be who God says we are and have what he says we have (6:11), the more these truths become our lived experience.

This sweeping overview of God's plan, this dramatic defense of God's wisdom throughout the ages, this revelation of a global salvation that began with one nation but extends to all who believe, made for a stunning unfolding of the plot in the first century—too stunning for many to accept. Two millennia later, it no longer surprises anyone familiar with the Christian faith. Perhaps we need to recapture the amazement of those who first believed. This gospel is still the power of God at work (1:16), and this new humanity is still emerging from a tired old world trapped in its own rebellion. The liberating message of this letter and the New Testament as a whole is the only answer to humanity's fundamental problem, and it's a glorious one. It restores us to the image we were once given, the image of God perfectly displayed in Jesus. And we can only receive it by faith.

To the degree that we live it by faith—as it sinks deep into our hearts, fills our vision, and becomes part of who we are—we no longer fall short of the glory of God.

Acknowledgments

Tracing one's own knowledge to its original sources is a nearly impossible task. I'm extremely grateful to have benefited from numerous sermons, lectures, commentaries, articles, essays, study materials, and personal conversations over the years, yet I can hardly remember any of them specifically. Our minds often work that way; they assimilate the information we receive and internalize it as "general understanding," as if we came to it ourselves, even when we know we didn't. So it is with my familiarity with Romans. I owe a debt to many influences I wish I remembered well enough to thank.

But I can at least acknowledge those whose works I consulted in preparation for writing this devotional commentary, including F. F. Bruce, Craig Keener, J. R. Daniel Kirk, David G. Peterson, Ben Witherington, N. T. Wright, and the unnamed scholars behind many reference notes. To these and many others, thank you for sharing your insights and expertise.

I am also grateful to the editorial team at Tyndale House Publishers, especially Dave Lindstedt for his careful and insightful work on this manuscript; as well as my agent, Mark Sweeney, for his encouragement and ever-reliable advice.

And, of course, I will forever be thankful for my wife, Hannah, and the rest of my family for their thoughtful questions, stimulating conversation, comic relief, enduring patience, and unwavering support.

May God fill the lives of all with blessing upon blessing.

Discussion Guide

This devotional commentary works well for individual use, but studying Scripture with other people and discussing biblical truths and insights is a great way to wrestle with and reinforce what you're learning. The following discussion prompts are organized into six manageable, thematic groupings to help get that conversation started. Feel free to condense these groupings into fewer sessions, divide them into more, or adapt them as you wish, depending on your needs and schedule. Do not feel compelled to discuss every question in every section. These are simply suggestions for touching on some of the most important themes of the book.

SESSION 1: INTRODUCTION AND ROMANS 1:1–3:20

1. Read Acts 9:15-16; 18:6; 22:17-21; 26:16-17; Romans 1:5, 13-14; 15:15-16. Based on these verses, how did Paul envision his mission? Who was he sent to reach? Why do you think Paul was inspired to write a letter to a church he had never visited?

2. Paul's statement in 1:17 that "it is through faith that a righteous person has life" (NLT) or "the righteous will live by faith" (NIV) can be read in multiple ways (see devotional on this verse). What are the implications of each of these different emphases? How might they affect how we read Romans?

3. How does Paul level the playing field for everyone, Jews and Gentiles alike, in these chapters? Why do you think he felt the need to do so? How do you think the original readers of this letter would have felt about his harsh assessment of the human condition?

4. Paul refers to the law both as a standard of righteousness and as a representation of Israel's special relationship with God. Why was it important to convey both of these meanings to his readers? What was at stake for Gentile believers, who didn't have this background with God, and for Jewish believers, who did?

5. What does Paul mean by "a true Jew is one whose heart is right with God" (2:29)? Read Deuteronomy 1:12-16; 30:6; and Jeremiah 4:4. How does Paul's reasoning reflect these passages? How does this set up what he will be presenting in the next few chapters?

SESSION 2: ROMANS 3:21–7:25

1. Paul has written much in the first three chapters about how the law has revealed unrighteousness, but also how God's righteousness has been revealed apart from the law. In what ways do Jesus and our faith in him show God to be righteous and just?

2. In what ways have we fallen short of God's glory (3:23)? As bearers of his image, what does this failure imply? What will it mean when the image is restored?

3. Read Genesis 15:1-6. According to this passage, what did Abraham believe about God? Why was he considered righteous? Why does the promise depend on faith (Romans 4:16)? Why is it important to Paul's argument that Abraham was declared righteous *before* he was circumcised?

4. What do you think Paul means by "peace with God" in 5:1-2? What does he mean by "undeserved privilege where we now stand"? Why is it important for us to see ourselves as undeservedly privileged—without apology, and to the full extent of God's generosity?

5. In what ways are Adam and Christ similar (chapter 5)? In what ways are they different? How does Paul explain the effects of each on the entire human race?

6. What does it mean to be baptized with Jesus in his death (6:3-11)? What does it mean to be raised with him? How does this image of death and resurrection change how we see ourselves?

7. How does being raised with Jesus set us free (6:15-23)? What does it set us free from? How can we experience this freedom practically?

8. Have you experienced the predicament of Romans 7 humanity (7:14-25)? If so, were you picturing yourself at the time as a sinner trying not to sin or as a righteous person transformed by God? How might the power of the Holy Spirit working within you have changed that experience?

SESSION 3: ROMANS 8

1. How does Paul's declaration of "no condemnation" and freedom (8:1-2) give us a new vision of ourselves? How do they relate to the struggle of the previous chapter?

2. According to 8:5-11, what does the Spirit of Christ enable us to do? What are the two mindsets Paul describes in this passage? What does this tell us about the importance of our thought life and our internal vision?

3. How does Paul's transition from the image of a slave to that of a child and heir change how we see God and relate to him (8:15-18)? How does being "heirs of God's glory" relate to the restoration of God's image within us? How does it empower us to live differently?

4. What is creation longing for (8:20-22)? How are its longings met in those who are being restored into God's image and inheriting his glory? Why do you think the revelation of new humanity (believers restored with God's image) is significant for God's work in this world?

5. What is the Holy Spirit's role in our prayers (8:26-27)? Do you picture him as praying *for* us, *with* us, *through* us, or all three? What is the outcome of these prayers?

6. The well-known promise of 8:28 has been read in different ways—as God causing the events and circumstances of our lives to eventually work out well for us (those who love him and are called according to his purpose), and as God working with us in our prayers (in 8:26-27) to work things out for good. How is each of these reassuring in its own way?

7. How does our transformation into the likeness of Jesus (8:29-30) summarize Paul's argument throughout Romans up to this point? How does it relate to the glory mentioned in 3:23, 5:2, and 8:17-18?

8. What are the implications of God being "for us" (8:31)? What are the implications of our "overwhelming victory" in Christ (8:37)?

SESSION 4: ROMANS 9–11

1. This passage of Romans contains more references to the Old Testament than any other passage of similar length in the New Testament. Why was it important for Paul to refer here to so many events, characters, and themes from Israel's history?

2. Many Christians think that God's plans in the Old Testament were all based on works, and now he has changed his plans and based everything on grace. How did Paul challenge this idea earlier (chapters 3–4) and now in chapter 9? What does Paul mean by "children of the promise" (9:8)?

3. In what ways has Jesus accomplished the purpose for which the law was given (10:4)?

4. How do Paul's words in 10:9-17 relate to missions and evangelism? How do they serve Paul's purpose in addressing friction between Jews and Gentiles and the role of the law in salvation history?

5. Many Christians throughout history have suggested that God has rejected Israel. How does Paul address this idea in chapter 11? Where does Israel (the historical people, not the modern nation) fit in God's current and future plans?

6. Paul begins this section with grief (9:1-3) but ends it with worship and praise (11:33-36). What led him to that conclusion?

SESSION 5: ROMANS 12:1–15:13

1. In what sense is becoming "a living and holy sacrifice" (12:1) the highest worship we can offer God? What are the implications of this offering for the way we think, speak, live, and relate to God and others? Why is renewing our minds an essential component of this sacrifice?

2. In chapter 12, Paul reorients our perspectives on God, the world, ourselves, other believers, and nonbelievers. How would you characterize these new perspectives? What's the bottom line that ties them together?

3. In what ways are believers interdependent? What does each of us have that other members of the body need?

4. Why do you think it was important for Paul to address our relationship to government in 13:1-7? If Christians declared Jesus (not Caesar) as Lord, how might some misunderstand the role of secular government in society—or the role of Christians within it?

5. How does love fulfill the law (13:8)?

6. How can we avoid causing other believers to stumble (14:13)? Does this mean we should cater to everyone's interpretation of righteous and unrighteous behavior? Why or why not?

7. What does Paul mean when he says that the Kingdom of God is not a matter of eating and drinking (14:17)? What does the Kingdom consist of? Why was it important for him to make these distinctions?

SESSION 6: ROMANS 15:14–16:27

1. Why do you think Paul reminded the Romans of his credentials (15:15-19)?

2. What was the role of signs and wonders in Paul's ministry (15:19)? In what ways does this demonstrate God's Kingdom and the new humanity?

3. Why do you think it was important for Paul to explain why he had not yet come to Rome (15:20-22)? How do you think Roman believers might have perceived this Jewish rabbi with a mission to Gentiles?

4. What do the greetings in 16:1-16 tell us about the relationships between early believers? In what ways did they span social boundaries? What sense of mission did they share? Do you think they expected the church to grow as it did? Why or why not?

5. What do you think it means that God "will soon crush Satan under your feet" (16:20)? What implications does this have for us today?

6. How has your understanding of Romans deepened over the course of reading it and meditating on it in depth? Has your vision of the Christian life—including God, yourself, the work of Jesus and the Holy Spirit, and life with other believers—changed? If so, how?

About the Author

CHRIS TIEGREEN has touched the lives of millions of people through his twenty-seven books, forty-plus study and discussion guides, many magazine and newspaper articles, and joint projects with other communicators. He has authored nine One Year devotionals, and his curricular and collaborative works have been translated into more than sixty languages, reaching many countries around the world. His experience in media, ministry, and higher education brings a unique perspective to his writing, which ranges from biblical teaching and devotional themes to cultural and historical commentary. Chris and his wife live in Atlanta.

NOTES